Twenty Easy Machine-Made Rugs

Other books in the Creative Machine Arts Series, available from Chilton:

Claire Shaeffer's Fabric Sewing Guide

The Complete Book of Machine Embroidery, by Robbie and Tony Fanning

Creative Nurseries Illustrated, by Debra Terry and Juli Plooster

Creative Serging Illustrated, by Pati Palmer, Gail Brown, and Sue Green

Distinctive Serger Gifts and Crafts, by Naomi Baker and Tammy Young

The Fabric Lover's Scrapbook, by Margaret Dittman

Friendship Quilts by Hand and Machine, by Carolyn Vosburg Hall

Innovative Serging, by Gail Brown and Tammy Young

Innovative Sewing, by Gail Brown and Tammy Young

Know Your Bernina, 2nd ed., by Jackie Dodson

Know Your Brother, by Jackie Dodson with Jane Warnick

Know Your Elna, by Jackie Dodson with Carol Ahles

Know Your New Home, by Jackie Dodson with Judi Cull and Vicki Lyn Hastings

Know Your Pfaff, by Jackie Dodson with Audrey Griese

Know Your Sewing Machine, by Jackie Dodson

Know Your Simplicity, by Jackie Dodson with Jane Warnick

Know Your Singer, by Jackie Dodson

Know Your Viking, by Jackie Dodson with Jan Saunders

Know Your White, by Jackie Dodson with Jan Saunders

Owner's Guide to Sewing Machines, Sergers, and Knitting Machines, by Gale Grigg Hazen

Petite Pizzazz, by Barb Griffin

Sew, Serge, Press, by Jan Saunders

Sewing and Collecting Vintage Fashions, by Eileen MacIntosh

Simply Serge Any Fabric, by Naomi Baker and Tammy Young

Thank You:

To my mother, Katherine Hanson, who has always inspired me. A rug-maker without equal, she piqued my interest in rugs years ago when she created floor coverings for every room in our home.

To Pat Welch for sharing her many rug ideas; Marilyn Tisol, my best critic and understanding friend, who checked to see if my directions made sense.

To my family, who put up with threads, scraps, and dust as a way of life, and especially to my granddaughters, Julie and Jennifer Molenda, who helped me tear, cut, and stack fabrics and kept me entertained during the most mundane tasks.

But especially to Robbie Fanning, for her optimism, encouragement, support, and friendship.

Twenty Easy Machine-Made Rugs

Jackie Dodson

Creative Machine Arts Series

Chilton Book Company
Radnor, Pennsylvania

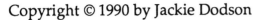

Published in Radnor, Pennsylvania 19089, by Chilton Book Company

Designed by Martha Vercoutere

Photography by Lee Phillips

Illustrations by Jackie Dodson

Manufactured in the United States of America

Library of Congress Cataloging in Publication Data

Dodson, Jackie.

      Twenty easy machine-made rugs / Jackie Dodson.

      147 p. cm. — (Creative machine arts series)

      Includes bibliographical references and index.

      ISBN 0-8019-8019-4 (pbk.)

      1. Rugs. 2. Machine sewing. I. Title. II. Series.

TT850.D63 1990   90-55323

746.7—dc20   CIP

1 2 3 4 5 6 7 8 9 0   9 8 7 6 5 4 3 2 1 0

Foreword

Some ideas in my life, perfectly obvious in afterthought, need a champion: making rugs on the sewing machine from scraps, for example. Why didn't I think of it myself? After all, 1) I have boxes and boxes of scraps too good to give away; 2) I love to sew; 3) I need rugs; 4) I can't afford to buy what I want.

But I didn't connect with machine-made rugs until Jackie Dodson sent me a charming denim rug to photograph for another of her books. The combination of old jeans used in such a fresh way opened my eyes to the possibilities. This book made them pop out of my head (e.g., cut up old Shetland sweaters, sew them onto a backing, unravel them—amazing!).

The idea of playing with color and texture in a non-threatening way is also enthralling. Somehow, spending a few evenings using up scraps in experimental color schemes for a throw rug is far less paralyzing than spending, say, a month using them in a quilt. If I don't like the result, I'll give it away without hesitation.

In fact, knowing that rugmaking by machine is easy and fast, my only remorse is that now I'll *never* be able to throw or give away a scrap. This book and Jackie Dodson will turn us all into rugged fabric packrats.

Robbie Fanning
Editor, Creative Machine Arts series

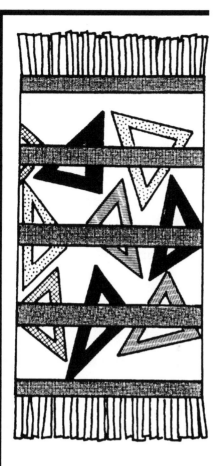

Contents

Introduction

I'm interested in any project that uses up my fabric scraps and yarn. That's because I collect fabric and yarn. Who am I kidding? Collect? Warehouse is more like it. I have boxes, trunks, and shelves full of three-yard (2.75m) lengths of fabrics and bags of yarn I *had* to have—fabric never used, sweaters that were only dreams. And I can't throw away even the tiniest scrap of fabric (what if I need that exact color someday?) or shred of yarn (I may need it for mending something).

Now, instead of hoping to use up my collection someday by making a thousand quilts or afghans for everyone in the family, I'm turning my stockpile into rugs. I can make rugs faster than I can make quilts or afghans, so where I used to give those to new babies and brides, now I'm going to make quilted bath mats to match towels for brides and choose favorites from this book to "wow" friends on special occasions.

If you love fabric, yarn, color, texture, and your sewing machine, you'll love creating rugs. Rugs are easy to make and hard to resist. My interest in rugs probably started 45 years ago when my mother first began making braided rugs. They seemed to take over our home. We couldn't ignore them—they were everywhere. Once too large to be braided on the table, the rug in progress was placed under the dining-room table to be finished. Rolls of wool fabric strips were in every empty corner. As soon as my mother's friends knew she braided wool rugs, clothing donations arrived with every visit and she could tell us about most of the wool in each rug—Pam's jackets, Jon's coat, a friend's sailor suit: her rugs were family histories. My rug making, too, feels like history repeating itself.

Part of the fascination of handmade rugs is that the rug maker incorporates so much of herself and her own personality into her work; her choices of color, fabric, texture, and design stamp the rug as her own. Like fingerprints, no two handmade rugs are ever exactly alike.

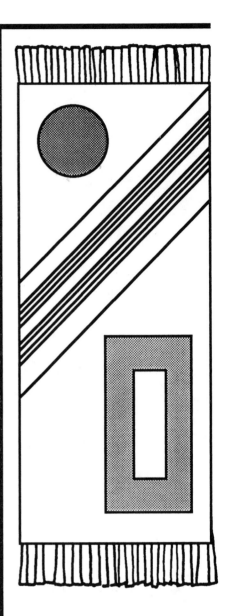

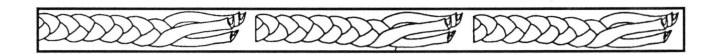

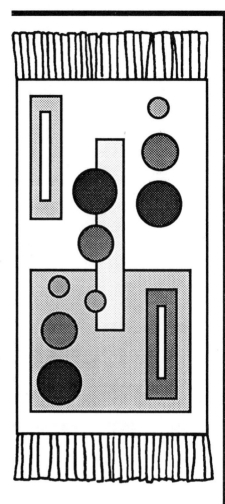

That's one of the reasons rug making is tailor-made for me and why I enjoy it so much. I like making original things, and this craft allows me the opportunity to experiment with three of my favorites— texture, color, and my sewing machine. (It's also an excuse to be a pack rat.) I especially like that there's no fitting necessary, so I don't have to be precise.

And it's a way to involve my family in my work (I'm not referring to the threads and scraps they slog through daily— in fact, I'm not going to discuss that at all). Many of us have children and grandchildren we want to interest in needlework because we know that to love needlework is never to be bored. But I hadn't thought of asking for help until our six-year-old granddaughters, who were vacationing with us, asked if they could make rugs with me. And did they help! They tore all the strips for the black Coiled Craft Cord Rug (with much laughing and crashing into furniture, as they each grabbed a side of the clip I'd made in the fabric and ran to opposite ends of the room). They also put all the colored scraps for the Amish Dust Catcher into separate plastic bags, then handed me the colors as I sewed the rug, taking precautions not to give me the same color twice-in-a-row. When I cut strips for the T-shirt rug, they pulled all the strips into tubes. We talked a lot, but this time it wasn't about friends or dresses; when they helped me with the rug, we talked about the colors and why they did or didn't like them, about textures (the Confetti Pompom Rug is a winner), and even about which designs they liked.

I prepared all these rugs for sewing (some vacation!), and the girls helped, in some way, with every rug. It was worth it. They haven't forgotten any of this experience; they enjoy pointing out sections of the rugs that remind them of something we did or said while making it. It's another family history.

Not only are these rugs a togetherness-craft, but I've found ways to do a great deal of the work while sitting comfortably in a favorite chair in the evening so I can be with my family, even if they don't help. In the directions for each rug I've indicated those times I have been able to relax and work on a rug at the same time. During the day I love to sew at my machine, but in the evening I want to be where the action is. After all, rug making should be fun, not tedious.

Rug making also should be inexpensive so you won't stop at making only one. If you don't have stacks of fabrics like I do, try garage sales, flea markets, and thrift shops. My mother and I used to buy wool skirts at thrift shops for her rugs, and I still find the best buys there in the fabric bins, in the curtain sections, or on shelves of aprons or clothing. If I don't find exactly the right colors, I may find something exciting enough to start me thinking of a new color combination for another rug. Sometimes I even find handmade rugs.

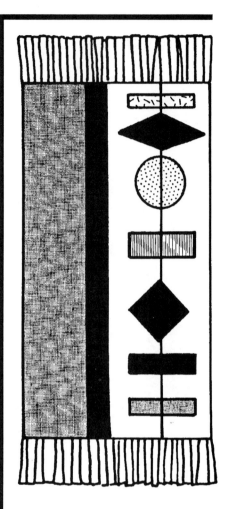

Thrift stores, garage sales, and flea markets offer out-of-print books and old magazines, as well, and needlepeople rank books right up there with fabric. I'm always on the lookout for old rug books or articles, and I've been collecting and saving rug information for years.

Without realizing it, my rug book began years ago, when I first started clipping and filing rug ideas. Soon my manila folder was inadequate for my burgeoning collection. I needed a file drawer; then it took over the whole file cabinet and our house, so I decided to get my files in order. As I did, it became apparent to me that there are only a few methods of making rugs, but the variations of those methods are limitless, and methods overlap. In my collection of books and clippings, I found rugs in every medium: knotting, knitting, hand embroidering, crocheting, weaving, quilting, machine stitching, and of course, rug hooking and braiding.

Except for coiling or quilting, I discovered that most machine-made rugs are appliquéd, because fabric or yarn is always sewn to a base. To organize my information, I arranged my book in this manner: After Chapter I (Getting Started), which is full of general information useful for all the rugs, I divided up the rugs into four chapters. Chapter II (Appliquéd and Embroidered Rugs) gives directions for

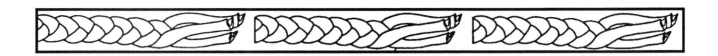

those rugs that are exclusively appliquéd or embroidered; Chapter III (Raveled, Fringed, and Looped) includes rugs made of yarn or fabric treated as yarn; Chapter IV (Coiled and Quilted) contains directions for the only two rugs that are not appliquéd; and Chapter V (Scraps and Strips) includes rugs made by cutting fabric scraps or strips. Finishing and caring for the rugs is included at the end of the book.

All of these rugs are either adaptations to the sewing machine of hand-sewn rugs (you'll be happy to know that machine-sewn rugs are much faster than the hand-sewn versions), old faithfuls that need no change, or my own inventions.

One of my prerequisites was that each rug be simple to make, so I looked for and included short-cuts and new twists to old methods.

Complicated designs were ruled out because learning the techniques is more important than struggling with complications. Once you learn the techniques, you can plan your rugs with your own fabric, thread, and color choices and know the joy of creating your own original rugs. You can also use the techniques on other items—garments, curtains, costumes, etc. I've given you ideas throughout the book.

You may think rug making goes hand-in-hand with sore shoulders and aching fingers and wonder what to do with all that bulk under the presser foot, or to the right of the needle. Yes, it's a pain for me, too, so I wasn't looking for short-cuts only; I experimented and found construction methods to eliminate the horror of bulk. You'll find my hints in the directions for each rug.

Now that all that's settled, what's stopping you? Get out your supplies and use these rug ideas for wall hangings, table runners, chair rugs, pillows, wearables, and, yes, even pet rugs. Soon you'll agree that all 20 of these rugs live up to the book's title—they're easy to make.

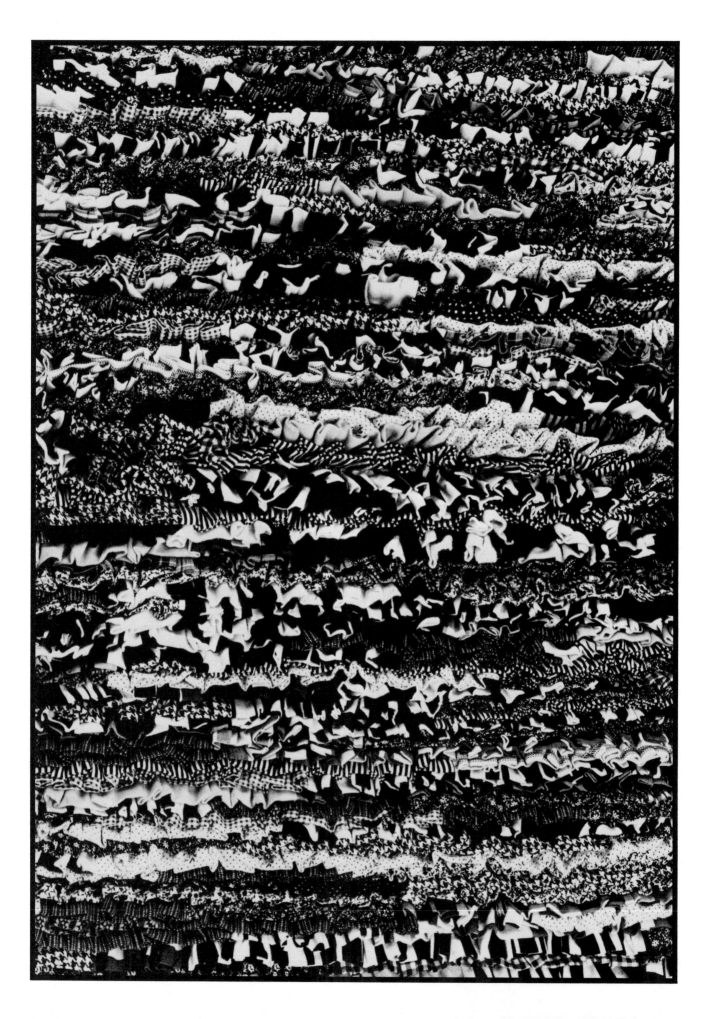

I. Getting Started

I f you have a zigzag machine that sews over thick layers of fabrics without skipped stitches, you can make these rugs. Work with your own color and fabric choices if you prefer; mine are only suggestions. But before you start making a rug, I suggest you work a 12-inch (30.5cm) sample first. Samples let you try a technique without investing too much money. Also, you'll learn how to use the fringe fork, how closely to sew the fabric scraps together, and how to estimate how much yardage you need for a rug.

Be sure you use compatible fabrics in your rug (all washable, for example) and always look to the future— how will the fabrics look after use? Begin by prewashing all the washable fabrics and backing you'll use.

The following is a shopping list of supplies to make the rugs found in this book. (The directions for each rug will give you a detailed materials list.) You probably have many of the supplies in your sewing room or you can order by mail (see Sources of Supplies at the end of the book).

1. Appliqué scissors; bent rug (also called machine embroidery) scissors (Figs. 1.1A and 1.1B); shears for cutting fabric; paper-cutting scissors; and short, sharp-pointed embroidery scissors.

2. Water-erasable and vanishing markers when lines will show on fabric; permanent, fine-line markers for lines that won't show.

3. 6" X 24" (15cm X 61cm) clear, plastic ruler.

4. Large-sized rotary cutter (Fig. 1.2) and mat (grid marked in 1" (2.5cm) squares and bias).

Fig. 1.1A

Fig. 1.1B

Fig. 1.2

Fig. 1.1 Use these scissors when making rugs.
  A. Trim fabric with the appliqué (Pelican) scissors.
  B. Use a curved rug (machine embroidery) scissors for trimming.
Fig. 1.2 Rotary cutters make fabric preparation easy.

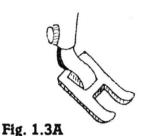

Fig. 1.3A

Fig. 1.3B

Fig. 1.3C

Fig. 1.3D

Fig. 1.3E

5. Presser feet:

    a. general purpose (zigzag).

    b. open embroidery (Fig. 1.3A).

    c. Bernina's knitter's or bulky overlock foot (fits Berninas only) (Fig. 1.3B).

    d. Elna's net curtain or no-snag foot (Fig. 1.3C), which is adaptable for any machine with the use of an adaptor shank. The foot is used for sewing looped surfaces and looks like an open embroidery foot with a bar across the end of the toes to keep the fabric loops from becoming entangled. It's possible to make your own by wrapping the toes of an embroidery foot with Magic Tape (Fig. 1.3D).

    e. cording (or wrap Magic Tape across the embroidery foot and punch a hole in the tape to accept and guide the cord) (Fig. 1.3E).

6. Jeans needles have pierce points; buy these in all sizes: #90/14, #100/16, #110/18, and #120/20.

7. Use polyester sewing threads or monofilament nylon for top and bobbin. Cordonnet by Metrosene is a thick, cordlike thread that fits in any needle size #110/18 or larger; gimp or #5 pearl cotton are sometimes preferred and can be used in place of cordonnet for gathering fabrics.

8. Drapery sash cord (braid) and roping; braids don't come apart easily, but roping does.

Fig. 1.3 The following presser feet are helpful in rug making:
    A. Open embroidery foot.
    B. Bernina's knitter's foot (bulky overlock).
    C. Elna's net curtain foot.
    D. Use Magic Tape to wrap toes to make a no-snag foot.
    E. Wrap toes with tape, then punch hole to make cording foot.

9. Fusible webbing such as Stitch Witchery or Wonder-Under can be used interchangeably unless indicated. Perky Bond and Stitch Witchery come in narrow, tape-like fusible strips. Use these when finishing a rug backing or cut off narrow strips from your yardage.

10. Teflon pressing sheet to use with fusible webbing.

11. Fringe forks come in various sizes. Buy them or make your own. To make a fringe fork, first decide how high you want the fringe. Will you stitch at one side? (Fig. 1.4A) Then make the fork the size of the fringe plus 1/4" (6mm) to allow for the thickness of the fork and stitches (I use a zipper foot and a tiny straight stitch). If you plan to stitch down the center of the fringe fork (Fig. 1.4B), double the height of the fringe plus 1/4" (6mm). For example, for fringe 1" (2.5cm) high, make the fringe fork twice this, or 2" (5cm) plus 1/4" (6mm) or 2-1/4" (5.7cm) wide.

When stitching down the center of the fringe fork, I use a medium-wide, short-length zigzag stitch, usually stitch width 3, stitch length 1, and a closed toe presser foot (Fig. 1.3B, C, or D) to keep the cords from tangling in it. A general purpose foot works, but it takes much more time to hold the yarn flat to the bed of the machine as you stitch over it. When sewing enough fringe for an entire rug, this could add up to hours of time.

Fringe feeds off end

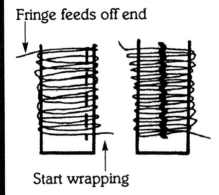

Start wrapping

Fig. 1.4A & B

Fig. 1.4
   A. Wrap the fringe fork and straight stitch down the side.
   B. Wrap the fringe fork and zigzag stitch down the center.

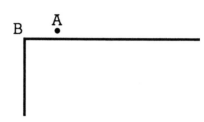

Fig. 1.5A

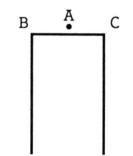

Fig. 1.5B

Fig. 1.5C

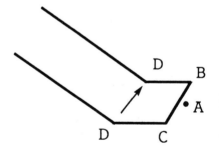

Fig. 1.5D

First find a heavy-duty metal clothes hanger and cut off the hook with a wire cutter or a hacksaw. Use pliers to straighten out the hanger (Fig. 1.5A). From the center of the wire, measure to the left half the width of the finished fork (Fig. 1.5B), and use pliers to bend the wire at a 90-degree angle. Next, measure from the center to the right and bend the wire 90 degrees (Fig. 1.5C). Let's call this rectangle of wire the front "curve". Finally, bend the front curve upward (Fig. 1.5D). (When wrapping the fork and stitching, the curve saves you hours of time as you never have to remove the fringe fork from the machine.)

12. Bonded batting, which holds together firmly, is used in the quilted rug.

13. Fray Check keeps edges from raveling.

14. Adding machine tape is used with a fringe fork for sewing long strips of yarn or fabric so that it doesn't twist.

15. Large safety pins, available at craft and quilt shops, are perfect for pin-basting the quilted bath mats.

Fig. 1.5 To make a 2" (5cm) fringe fork:
A. Straighten heavy wire and mark mid-point (A).
B. Bend wire at a 90 degree angle 1" (2.5cm) from mid-point (B).
C. Repeat at other side of mid-point (C).
D. Bend up front 1-1/2" (4cm) to make winding yarn easier (D).

Helpful hints for sewing:

1. When I designate a stitch width or length such as 3 or 2, I'm referring to millimeters. Most computer machines are preset to stitch 3.5 or 1.8, for example, so use the setting closest to the one I use. Check your manual if you're not sure, or stitch a sample of stitch widths and lengths. Then measure the stitches.

2. Heavy fabrics such as canvas or striped pillow ticking are the most useful backing fabrics. Always prewash and press. Whenever the backing won't show, then use striped ticking. This has been used through the ages to keep lines of stitching straight. If you have neither, then fuse together two pieces of lighter-weight fabric.

3. Clean your machine often. Take the throat plate off and brush out the lint caught in the feed dogs. After the inside has been freed of lint, put a drop of oil in every spot that needs lubricating.

4. Stitch up rug modules and combine them into a larger rug if the weight or size of the rug is too great to work on comfortably.

5. Depending on the size and weight of your rug, pull your sewing table or cabinet away from the wall. Pull up another table to the left or in back of your cabinet, if possible, to keep the rug from pulling away from the needle.

6. To eliminate broken needles, let the machine feed the rug under the needle, despite the temptation to pull on bulky layers. Hand-walk the presser foot, if needed, by turning the handwheel. Sometimes setting the stitch length longer will keep the rug feeding smoothly under the presser foot.

Appliquéd and Embroidered

- Snowflake Rug
- Tongues and Shoe Heels Welcome Mat
- Cheater's Rug
- Buttonhole and Rope Rug

II. Appliquéd and Embroidered

If you love machine stitchery, as I do, then these four rugs are naturals for you.

The Snowflake Rug is made of heavy blanket material with wool appliqués and yarn outlines. The feel of the soft wool made it a sewing favorite of mine.

Perhaps you've only satin stitched appliqué edges and you've never sewn yarn around an appliqué as I show in the Snowflake Rug, but try it. I have an aversion to heavy satin stitches around an appliqué and I think you'll like this alternative as much as I do.

Directions for using it on the floor or wall are included. If you make a wall hanging, try using felt instead of wool for easy construction.

The Tongues and Shoe Heels Welcome Mat is a descendant of the first rag rugs made of worn-out clothing scraps which were overlapped and sewn to a backing. Instead of being purely useful, as they once were, the rugs are now more for decorative purposes. (On the other hand, isn't decoration a use?)

Couching down cord (Cheater's Rug) isn't new, but it is a fast way to brighten up an otherwise everyday rug. Use designs from coloring books for children's rooms, or use nursery catalogs for flower designs, use quilt books for quilting patterns, or use your imagination.

The Buttonhole and Rope Rug came about when I practiced couching down thick cords while experimenting with my new sewing machine. I used the buttonhole stitch over the cord and it reminded me so much of weaving, I had to pursue it. The Rope Rug was born and I was pleased with the results.

An excellent table rug, it has a flat, but intriguing surface ("How was this made?"), and you can use any thread colors to match your decor. Use it wherever you want to add a bit of interest and a touch of color—over a trunk or on top of a dresser. The dimensions can be anything you choose for a custom look. I made a narrow table runner for our old, oak kitchen table.

1. Snowflake Rug

In the Midwest we begin checking weather reports by the end of November to see if we can expect snow for Christmas. I love snow, and now I have this rug to remind me of it even if it never appears.

Rug size: 33" X 51" (.8m X 1.5m)

Stitch width: 1 – 3

Stitch length: 1-1/2 to 2

Needle: #90/14 jeans

Thread: top and bobbin, white polyester and monofilament

Presser foot: open embroidery or clear, plastic appliqué foot

Fabric: 36" X 54" (.9m X 1.5m) red coating or blanket weight and 24" X 54" (61cm X 1.5m) white dress-weight wool (**Note:** I made one snowflake each 18" (46cm) square, 9" (23cm) square, 5" (13cm) square; two snowflakes 12" (30.5cm) square); 36" X 54" (.9m X 1.5m) green felt

Yarn: several weights of white wool

Miscellaneous: notebook paper cut into squares of various sizes, paper and fabric scissors, embroidery scissors, Wonder-Under fusible webbing, appliqué scissors (optional), black, fine-line permanent marker, dressmaker's pins, hand-sewing needle

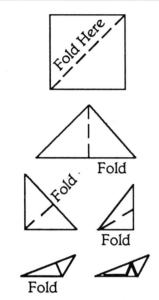

Fig. 2.1

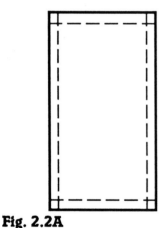

Fig. 2.2A

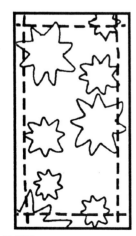

Fig. 2.2B

Using the paper squares to make paper patterns for the wool appliqué snowflakes, fold and cut many design samples to find the ones you can use for the rug (Fig. 2.1). The first ones I cut were gorgeous, lace-like snowflakes, which would be lovely on my rug—but not practical to make. Intricate, tiny cut-out areas meant extra hours, perhaps days of stitching. So instead, I cut out large, less complicated snowflakes to use for the wool appliqués. After deciding which large snowflakes to use, I also cut out medium-sized flakes, then smaller ones. If you have one design you especially like, you may make all the snowflakes the same.

Later, to give the look of more airy, lacelike flakes, outline several of the paper cut-outs in white wool yarn without fabric.

Using monofilament in top and bobbin, begin by straight stitching around the red fabric, 1-1/2" (4cm) from each edge to mark the border (Fig. 2.2A). Arrange the paper snowflakes on the back of the red fabric, placing some of them slightly beyond the stitched border (Fig. 2.2B). Is the arrangement pleasing? Decide which appliqués you'll use, which you'll eliminate. Remember to visualize how the yarn flakes will look and where they'll be placed. Overlap yarn snowflakes with appliqués, if you wish. Pin the patterns in place and then, with a permanent marker, draw all around the patterns (remember, this is the back of the red fabric and the marker won't show on the front). Include the yarn snowflakes as well. If you feel the yarn snowflakes need a few more lines inside them, feel free to change them at this time.

Fig. 2.1 An example of how to fold and cut squares of paper to make snowflakes.

Fig. 2.2
  A. Straight stitch 1-1/2" (3cm) from the edge around the red fabric.
  B. Arrange the snowflakes, placing some of them slightly beyond the straight-stitched border.

Take the snowflakes off the red fabric and place them onto the back of a sheet of Wonder-Under fusible webbing. Trace around them. Press the Wonder-Under to the back of the white wool fabric, then cut between the snowflakes. (Don't cut out the snowflake designs yet.)

Place the red fabric, topside down, on the bed of the machine. Then stitch with white thread on top and in the bobbin, following the marker lines drawn on the rug for only the yarn snowflakes. Turn the fabric over; the design is now stitched on top. This is the stitching guide. Using the white yarn you've chosen, with monofilament on the bobbin and top, you will couch the yarn down, following the design stitched in white thread. If you wish, use different weights of yarn for some of the snowflakes to give the rug depth and variety. I used medium-weight boucle, sport weight, and worsted.

Leave a tail of yarn at the beginning to hold as you begin, or push it down through the red wool before stitching (Fig. 2.3A). I found it simple to zigzag (use a stitch width that covers the cord, a stitch length that leaves yarn showing—stitch width 3, stitch length 1-1/2). When you finish a pass, overlap the yarn already couched in place (Fig. 2.3B) and anchor the thread by sewing in one place several times, clipping the yarn back to the anchor stitches. You can push all yarn ends to the back of the rug, but I found that to be unnecessary.

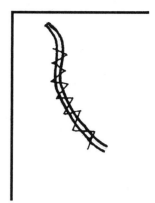

Fig. 2.3A

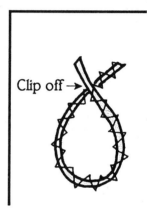

Clip off →

Fig. 2.3B

Fig. 2.3
   A. Poke to the back or leave a tail of yarn at the beginning of the appliqué.
   B. Overlap the yarn and anchor, then clip back to finish.

Chapter II **Appliquéd and Embroidered 11**

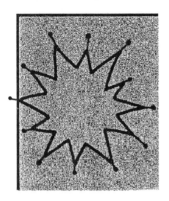

Fig. 2.4A

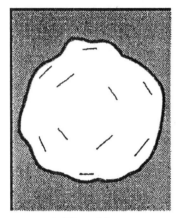

Topside

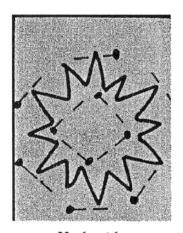

Underside

Fig. 2.4B

Once the yarn snowflakes are in place, find the snowflakes of white wool fabric you put aside. Again, working with the topside of the rug down, place dressmaker's pins around the outside of the marked outline of the first snowflake you'll appliqué (Fig. 2.4A). Then turn the rug over carefully, pull off the Wonder-Under backing, and place the wool piece that covers this area over the pins—fusible webbing facing the rug (Fig. 2.4B). Pin the wool in place from the underside; remove the other pins. Place the rug on the machine, underside on top, and straight stitch around the design, following the marker outlines.

Continue applying the white fabric pieces in the same way until all of the fabric for the white appliques is in place. Turn the rug over. The white wool is attached to the rug and the designs are outlined. With appliqué scissors or small, pointed embroidery scissors, clip back to the stitching at the edges and cut open the areas of one appliqué. Now take the rug to the ironing board and fuse this snowflake in place. Next, couch down yarn at the edges of the design as you did the yarn snowflakes (stitch width 3, stitch length 1-1/2). Use monofilament on top and bobbin. Proceed with the next appliqué. Cut back one appliqué at a time to prevent their pulling away from the straight stitching as you jockey the rug around under the presser foot.

By finishing the edges of the appliqués with couched yarn instead of satin stitching, the results are more attractive, easier to stitch, and a stabilizer isn't needed under the work because the stitches are so far apart the fabric won't ripple.

When finished, take the rug off the machine and place it on the floor. Look at it. Do you need more snowflake outlines? More appliqués? Now is the time to add them.

Fig. 2.4
A. Place dressmaker's pins around the marked outline of the snowflakes.
B. Place white wool on the topside, between pins. Pin in place from the underside.

The backing goes on next. Cut the green felt the same size as the red fabric—36" X 54" (.9m X 1.5m). Using monofilament in top and bobbin, mark the borders by stitching 1-1/2" (4cm) from the edge across the top and bottom (Fig. 2.5). Place topside of the rug against the backing and pin them together. Following the stitching lines on the red wool, stitch the backing to the rug at both long sides, beginning and ending at the stitched borders at top and bottom (Fig. 2.6). Finger press toward the back. Go back and stitch down seam allowances 1/8" (3mm) from the seam, toward the back (Fig. 2.7). Cut the green felt seam allowances back to 1/4" (6mm) wide and turn the rug right-side out.

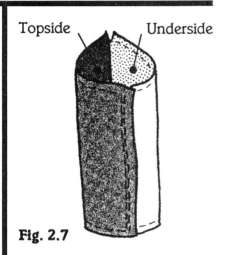

Topside   Underside

Fig. 2.7

Fig. 2.5

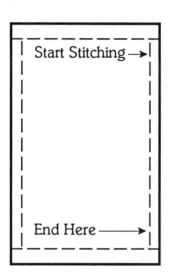

Fig. 2.6

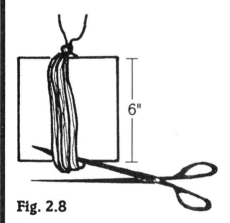

Fig. 2.8

Fig. 2.5 Stitch 1-1/2" (4cm) from top and bottom edges of the backing.

Fig. 2.6 Attach front to back from straight-stitched borders at top and bottom.

Fig. 2.7 Stitch down seam allowance toward back.

Fig. 2.8 Wrap tassel over a 6"-long (15cm) piece of cardboard.

Now gather up all the different types of yarn you used in the rug and make 34 plump 6"-long (15cm) tassels. I used a tassel maker (see Sources of Supplies), but you can cut a piece of cardboard 6" (15cm) wide, wrap the cardboard, tie at the top and clip the yarn from the cardboard at the bottom (Fig. 2.8). Wrap the top to finish the tassel as shown in Figure 2.9.

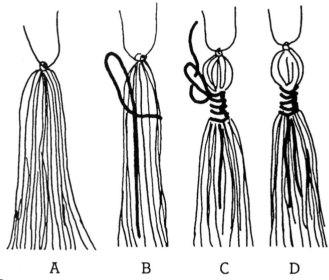

A   B   C   D

Fig. 2.9

Next, place the rug on a flat surface and arrange the tassels 2" (5cm) apart across the top and bottom edges (17 tassels at each edge) (Fig. 2.10), ends facing toward the center of the rug. Pin the knots at the top of the tassels to the rug's top stitching line (don't catch in the backing). Take the rug to the machine and stitch the tassels in place, stitching on top of the straight stitching already there.

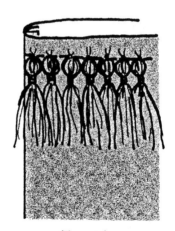

Topside

Fig. 2.10

Fig. 2.9
    A. Tie cords together at the top.
    B. Place wrapping cord next to tassel, loop at top.
    C. Wrap from bottom up around the tassel and place end of yarn through loop. Pull down on the other end of wrapping cord to bring loop down, inside of wrap.
    D. Clip end.

Fig. 2.10 Pin the tassels, at the knots, to the line of straight stitching at top and bottom of the rug.

Take the rug off the machine and fold in the borders on the stitching lines at top and bottom. Hand stitch in place for a clean look (Fig. 2.11), or machine stitch across if you desire.

I prefer using a ladder stitch to sew the opening shut because the stitches are hidden completely in the folds at the ends of the wall hanging (Fig. 2.12).

Begin by threading your needle and knotting the end of the thread. Poke the needle up from the back on one side, then out on top. Stitch directly across and through the edge of the fold on the other side. Then slip the needle along under the fold for approximately 1/4" (6mm) and again poke it out of the folded edge and into the edge directly across on the other side. To keep the sides snugged up to each other, pull up on the stitches as you proceed. Continue this ladder stitch till the opening is stitched closed. (No, you can't see any stitches.)

Wall hangings get so little wear and tear that their construction doesn't have to be as sturdy as rugs.

Felt is often the fabric of choice because no edge finish is needed on cut felt. You have several options when attaching a felt appliqué. One of the easiest is to apply felt pieces with fusible webbing between appliqué and backing, and then straight stitch at the edge around the appliqué to hold it in place permanently. Yes, you can use glue stick to hold the appliqué while stitching, but glue can't hold the edges in place like fusibles do, so the appliqué usually creeps into pleats as you stitch it down. However, if you must use glue, go easy—use light sweeps of the glue stick to prevent globs and lumps, which can show through the appliqué and look dreadful.

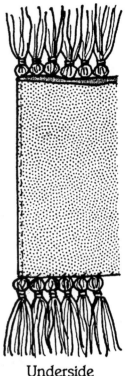

Underside

Fig. 2.11

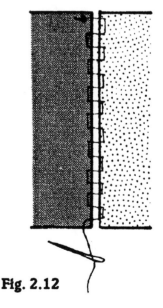

Fig. 2.12

Fig. 2.11 Fold top and bottom edges to the inside at the stitching lines and hand stitch closed.

Fig. 2.12 Ladder stitch the rug together by hand.

Chapter II **Appliquéd and Embroidered** **15**

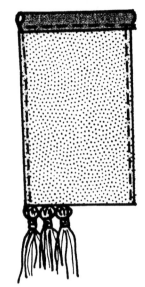

Fig. 2.13A

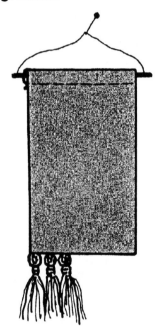

Fig. 2.13B

After fusing the appliqués in place, an alternative to straight stitching is an almost invisible application, using either the buttonhole stitch (Fig. 2.19) or blind-hem stitch (Fig. 2.20). Use monofilament thread on top, and sewing thread on the bobbin the same color as the backing. Adjust the stitch width to take short bites on the stitch swings that attach the appliqué to the backing. Sew around at the side, off the appliqué. Only the wide swing of the needle tacks the appliqué down.

Of course you can attach the felt appliqués more decoratively by using the same method I used for the wool snowflakes and couch down yarn around them.

If you're doing a quickie wall hanging—decorating for a party, for example, or even for the Christmas season—you can fuse the snowflakes to the wall hanging and not sew a stitch. But this is only temporary. If you plan to use the wall hanging again, then stitch the appliqués in place permanently. You'll be glad you did.

Fig. 2.13
  A. Fold over the top edge at the straight stitching, creating a sleeve.
  B. Slip dowel through the top sleeve for hanging.

Attach the topside to the backing as you did for the rug, but instead of starting 1-1/2" (4cm) from the top, stitch to the top at both sides. Fold toward the back on the 1-1/2" (4cm) line at the top (both red and green) and stitch across by machine on top of the raw edges to create a sleeve (Fig. 2.13A). It's unnecessary to finish the edge any more than this because felt doesn't fray, and the red wool is thick and tightly woven. Finish the bottom with tassels. Slip a dowel through the top sleeve for hanging (Fig. 2.13B).

Further thoughts and ideas: Once I began to appliqué this rug, I could see this technique used for other home decor (valances, pillows, window treatments) as well as for clothing. Apply glitzy fabrics with glitzy threads or velveteens with velour yarn (it looks like an extension of the velveteen and is one of my favorite discoveries), or use cottons with a pearl cotton thread around the edges. Invent your own fabrics by eliminating the appliqués and couching down cords in all-over patterns (I couched down threads following some of the lines of color in a marbleized fabric). We've all seen soutache braid used on clothing, but try a freer look—use thick or thin, smooth or fuzzy cords and yarn to add a passementerie touch.

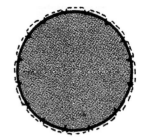

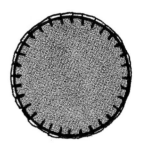

Fig. 2.14

Fig. 2.14 Attach appliqués using a blind hem or buttonhole stitch.

Chapter II **Appliquéd and Embroidered 17**

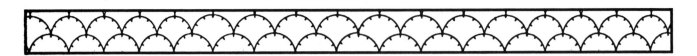

2. Tongues and Shoe Heels Welcome Mat

Fig. 2.15

Tongues, fish scales, shoe heels, petals, pen wipers, and pennies are all names for this type of appliquéd rug. There seem to be as many styles to these rugs as there are rug makers making them. Originally a hearth or table rug, it's still best to keep them out of heavily trafficked areas.

Fig. 2.15 Arrange tongues in this formation.

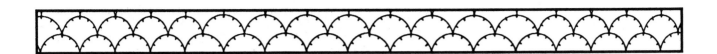

Rug size: 25" X 36" (64cm X .9m)

Stitch width: 0 – widest

Stitch length: satin stitch – 2

Needle: #90/14 jeans

Thread: red, bright blue, navy blue machine-embroidery cotton

Presser foot: open embroidery foot

Fabric: 1 yard (.9m) each red, bright blue, navy blue, plaid wool (this is contingent on using self-fabric for linings and matching plaid); (Lay out patterns first to estimate yardage you'll need (Fig. 2.16).) Two pieces 28" X 40" (71cm X 1m) wool backing fabric

Yarn: 1 yard (.9m) red sport-weight yarn

Miscellaneous: tapestry needle; fusible webbing; red, bright blue, navy blue #5 pearl cotton; tear-away stabilizer or construction paper to match thread; tracing paper; red, blue, and black permanent markers; 7" X 15" (18cm X 38cm) piece of bonded batting; 6" X 24" (15cm X 61cm) clear plastic ruler; Fray Check or glue stick (optional); two pieces of paper or fabric larger than rug; ruler; 18 black self-stick Velcro dots (optional); 28" X 40" (71cm X 1m) stiff black buckram (optional)

Above: Tongues and Shoe Heels Rugs are used away from traffic areas.

Rugs in this color section:

Machine-Made Rugs

Above: Quickly stitch up a rug using lengths of upholstery fringe.

Right: Use the wool Snowflake Rug to decorate the wall or the floor.

Machine-Made Rugs

Machine-Made Rugs

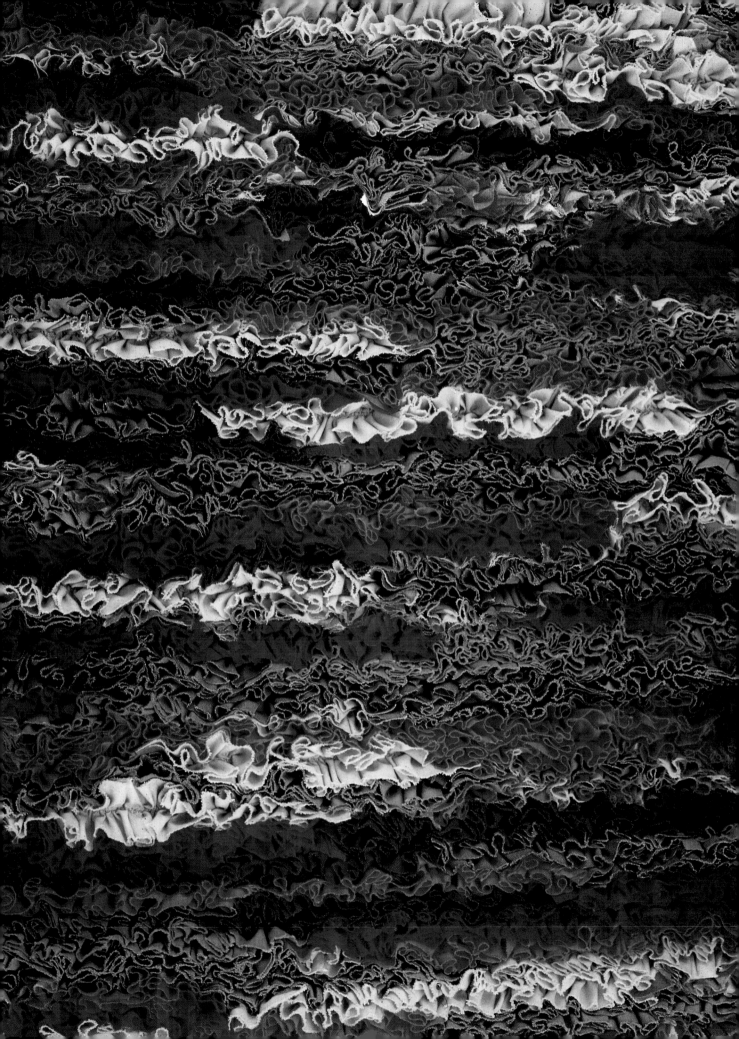

Above: *Decorate commercially woven throw rugs in an instant.*

Left: *Colors chosen for the Carmen Miranda Rug match those in the striped fabric used.*

Machine-Made Rugs

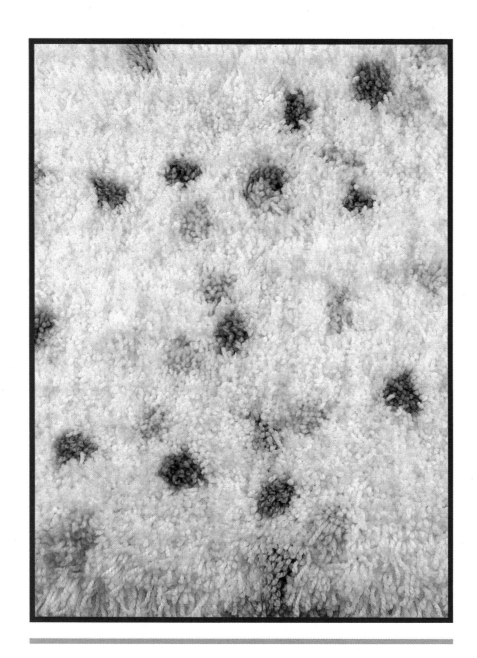

Above: Pompoms sewn in rows create a luxurious texture.

Right: Squares folded into triangles are arranged like butterflies on this rug.

Machine-Made Rugs

Above: *Overlap rectangles of fabric to make an Amish Dustcatcher.*

Machine-Made Rugs

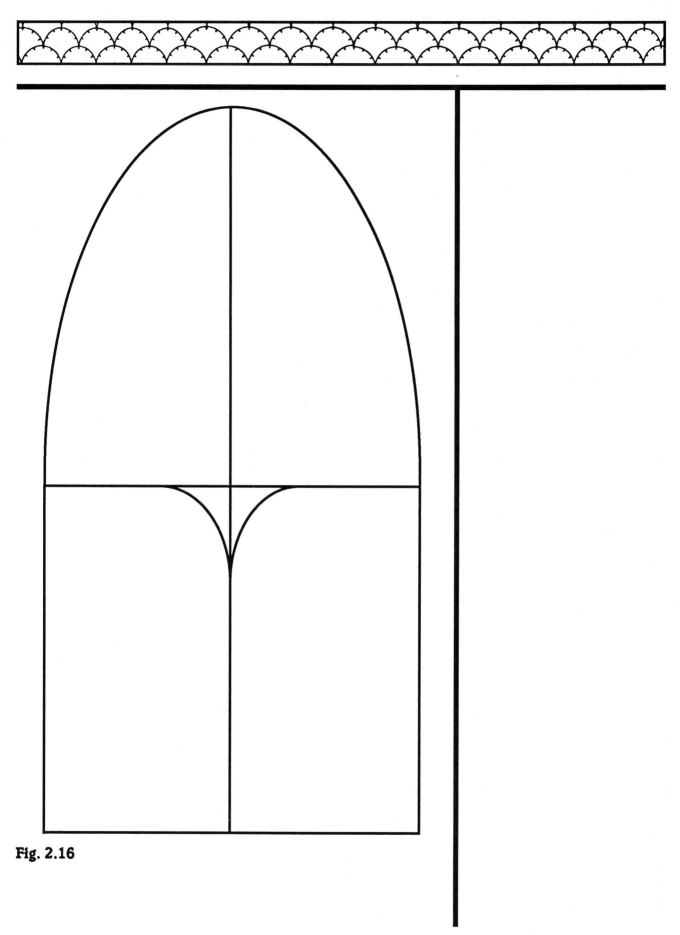

Fig. 2.16

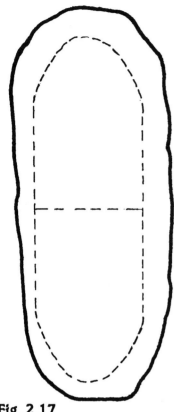

Fig. 2.17

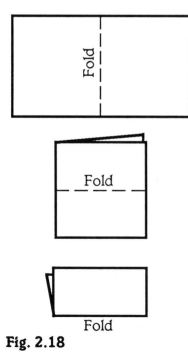

Fig. 2.18

It was difficult to find blanket or coat woolens in the bright colors I wanted, so I solved the problem by buying twice as much fabric as I needed and fusing two layers of light-weight wool together. I did this to prevent the outlines of the tongues underneath from shadowing through the row of tongues on top of it.

To fuse fabrics, I placed a layer of wool on the ironing board (topside down), a sheet of fusible webbing on top, then another layer of wool (topside up), and I pressed these in place to fuse them together. You can use any color underneath any of the tongues as long as it doesn't show through and alter the color of the top layer.

You'll need 12 plaid tongues (six oval patterns) (Fig. 2.17), 14 red (seven ovals), 16 bright blue (eight ovals), and 18 navy blue (nine ovals). Also, cut out a piece of navy fabric, 7" X 15" (18cm X 38cm), for the center. To prepare the center, fold the fabric in half, then in half the other way, and round off the corner points (Fig. 2.18). You need only one of these.

Using the oval template allows you to produce two tongues at one time. You will finish the edges of each oval, then cut them in half. Trace around the oval template the number of times specified in the last paragraph. Space the ovals about 1/2" (1.5cm) from each other. Then cut around

Fig. 2.17 An oval pattern is made by placing two tongues together.

Fig. 2.18 Fold the center rectangle into fourths, then round off the outside corners (not shown).

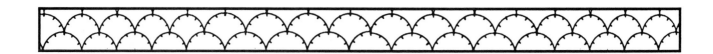

each pair 1/4" (6mm) outside the marker line and straight stitch around the ovals on the marker lines. Next, cut the fabric back to one or two threads from the stitching line (you will satin stitch the edge).

Place each oval set of tongues on stabilizer or construction paper. Decide what color of thread you'll use to finish the edge, because you'll want the construction paper color to match. (My thread color choices for the tongues are: plaid tongues, red thread; red tongues, bright blue thread; bright blue tongues, navy thread: navy blue tongues, red thread.) If you stitch with red thread, use red construction paper, blue thread, blue construction paper, etc. Using the open embroidery foot, cording foot, or any presser foot that will accommodate the widest stitch width, stitch around the edge with any stitch on your machine that imitates a handmade buttonhole stitch (Fig. 2.19). Be sure it faces toward the inside of the tongue, or use mirror image, if you have it. I set mine on the longest stitch length, and widest stitch width. If you don't have a buttonhole stitch on your machine, use a blind hem at a wide setting (Fig. 2.20). You also can use a zigzag stitch set slightly longer and narrower than the final pass (use stitch width 3, stitch length 3/4). I always satin stitch with a jeans or pierce point needle. This way the needle pokes through the fabric where it should; it doesn't search for a space between threads as the universal needle does; and my satin stitch edges are crisp and unwavering.

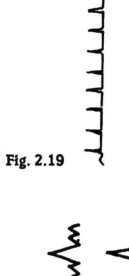

Fig. 2.19

Fig. 2.20

Fig. 2.19 Use a "buttonhole" stitch for tongue edges.

Fig. 2.20 Use one of these blind-hem examples as a substitute "buttonhole" stitch.

Chapter II **Appliquéd and Embroidered 23**

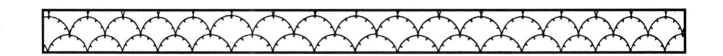

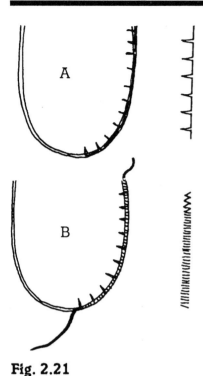

A

B

Fig. 2.21

After stitching, tear away any stabilizer that is still under the tongue. On the final pass, use a satin stitch setting over the edge. The widest stitch-swings of the buttonhole stitch are still visible, but the edge is covered on this pass (Fig. 2.21).

Place a piece of #5 pearl cotton at the edge as you satin stitch around the oval. Set the satin stitches approximately half as wide as the buttonhole stitches (this will depend on your machine settings). The satin stitch should wrap and cover the edge smoothly, with stitches close together. I set my machine on stitch width 3, stitch length set for satin stitch setting. After all the ovals are stitched the same way, cut them apart on the center lines to make tongues.

When stitching is completed, go back with a permanent marker the color of the thread and color the edges if the fabric or stabilizer is still visible between the stitches.

Next, place the center of the rug on tear-away or red construction paper and stitch "buttonhole stitches" around the perimeter first. Then go back and stitch satin stitches at the edge with pearl cotton, as before.

Choose a greeting for the center. I opted for something simple: "Welcome." In fact, I chose the lettering style—it looks almost childlike—from a magazine article about hearth

Fig. 2.21
A. On the first pass, buttonhole stitch around edges of the tongues.
B. On the last pass, satin stitch over pearl cotton.

rugs. Cut a piece of tracing paper the size of the center of the rug. Then print the letters within the limits of the paper. Once the spacing is acceptable, place the tracing paper over the navy blue rug center, and with the machine set on a short, straight stitch (stitch length 1-1/2), stitch through the letters with red thread on the top. This transfers the lettering to the fabric. The tracing paper drops away when finished. The letters are stitched by zigzagging over red sport-weight yarn to raise them slightly. For each letter, poke a needle and the red yarn up through the back of the fabric at the beginning of the letter, leaving a 1/2" (1.5cm) tail underneath. Then draw the yarn to the ending point and poke the needle through to the back (Fig. 2.22A and 2.22B). Each letter except "E" is accomplished with one piece of yarn. Hold the yarn taut and zigzag over it, setting the stitch width to cover the yarn. The length should be set on approximately stitch length 1.

Go back over the yarn, this time stitching slightly wider and much shorter stitches than the first. I used stitch width 4, stitch length set for satin stitching. Use Fray Check or a dab of glue stick on the back at the starts and stops. Clip threads.

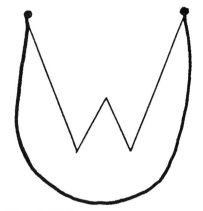

Fig. 2.22A

Fig. 2.22B

Fig. 2.22
   A. Push cord through to back at both ends of the letter.
   B. Zigzag stitch the cord in place.

Chapter II **Appliquéd and Embroidered** **25**

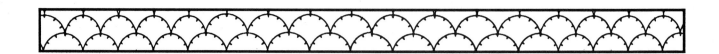

Fuse the two backing pieces together with a piece of fusible webbing. It covers the entire back of the finished rug. Because there are variables when making this rug—even if you follow the directions—be sure the backing is large enough. The rug is 24" X 36" (61cm X .9m). Make the backing at least 28" X 40" (71cm X 1m), then put it aside.

The only way to build this rug is from the center out; however, it's stitched from the outside in. Therefore, you will work on a flat surface and do a lot of flipping under and over, off and on. It sounds harder than it is.

Place a piece of fabric or paper (larger than the finished rug measurement) on the table. This will help you position the tongues and turn the rug over. Place the welcome sign in the center of the paper. Then slip the plaid tongues in place under the center piece. Use a ruler to see that the tongues protrude the same distance from the center on each side and at the ends. It's easiest to start at the straight sides first, then the straight tongues at each end. Slip the corner, slanted tongues under last. Pin them all to the center rectangle but not to the paper.

After pinning the plaid tongues in place, the red ones are next. Place them under the plaid pieces in a shingle-like arrangement. Measure and pin to the first row of tongues, but not to the paper. Slip blue tongues under the red as pictured; measure and pin. Finally, place and pin the navy blue tongues under the previous row.

Once the rug is arranged and pinned together, place another piece of fabric or paper over the entire rug (don't use the backing fabric). Use the paper underneath to help flip the rug over so it is upside down. Remove the first fabric or paper you used underneath (it is now on top) and replace it with the wool backing. Smooth and pin the backing in place only around the outside edge. Again, flip the rug over.

Unpin and take the center piece off the rug and slip batting under it, making sure none of it shows beyond the edge. Pin it in place to the plaid tongues again, without pinning through the backing. Unpin the backing and last row of navy tongues from the rest of the rug. Then carefully take off the rest of the rug in one piece and set it aside. Pin the navy tongues to the backing (Fig. 2.23). Use the color of the backing in the bobbin and use monofilament on top, or choose the same color of the thread used for satin stitching around the

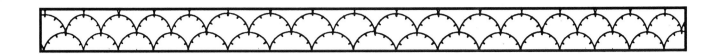

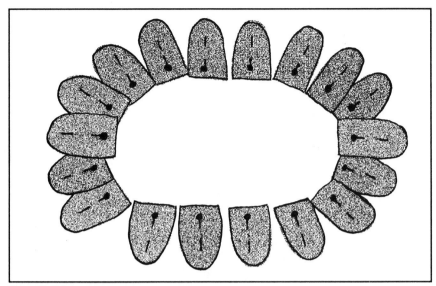

Fig. 2.23

tongues. Straight stitch (stitch length 2) around each tongue at the inside edge of the satin stitches and continue across the straight end on each piece to attach the tongues to the backing.

When finished with the navy blue row of appliqués, position the rest of the rug over the navy blue tongues in correct alignment. Pin the bright blue tongues to the navy blue row and unpin them from the rest of the rug. Lift off the top of the rug as one piece and set it aside. Stitch the bright blue tongues in place as you did the first row. Go back and place the rug top over the blue tongues again. Position it, then pin the red tongues in the proper places and unpin from the rest of the rug. Do the same with the last, plaid row. Finish by stitching down the welcome sign center piece.

Turn the rug over and trim the backing fabric slightly back from the satin stitches of the navy tongues so the backing doesn't show from the front, and leave the edge as it is, or touch Fray Check around the raw edge.

The next step is optional: To keep the back clean and the stitches from wearing, cut a piece of stiff black buckram approximately the same size as the rug, and slip it underneath. Then press self-stick dots of Velcro at the ends of the scallops and directly under them on the buckram. Carefully, cut out the shape of the rug from the buckram underneath it. This not only protects the back of the rug, but helps keep the last row of tongues from curling.

Fig. 2.23 Take the rest of the rug off the last row of tongues.

Chapter II **Appliquéd and Embroidered 27**

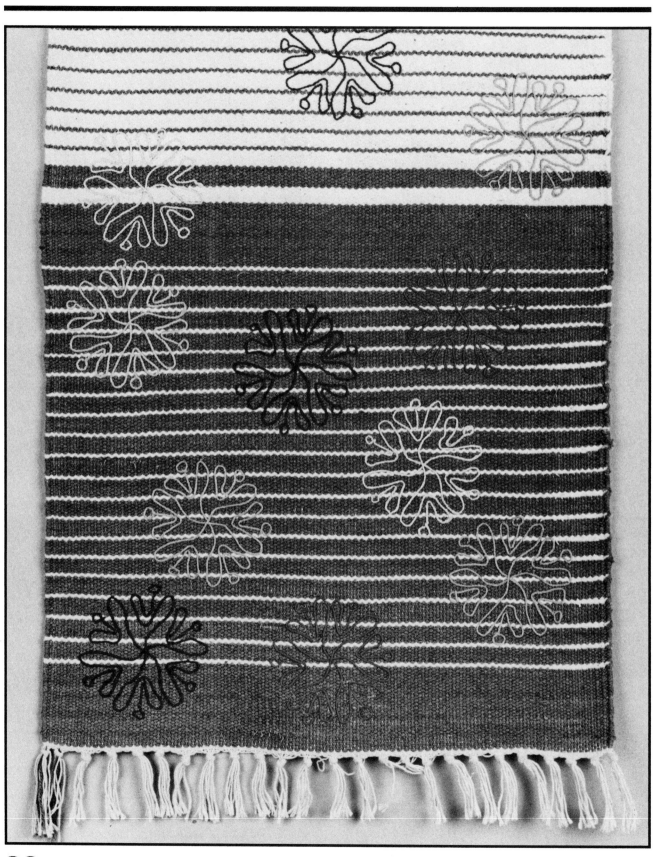

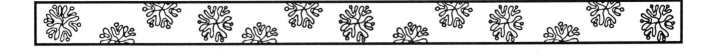

3. Cheater's Rug

Cheater's is a good name for this rug. You have to couch down the flower designs yourself, but once they are in place, the rug is finished because it starts with a commercially made, woven rug.

I found the green striped, woven rug at a Ben Franklin for less than $10. It had possibilities. It also matched our kitchen, so how could I go wrong? And while poking around the needlework department in the same store, I found all the yarn I needed in all the right colors.

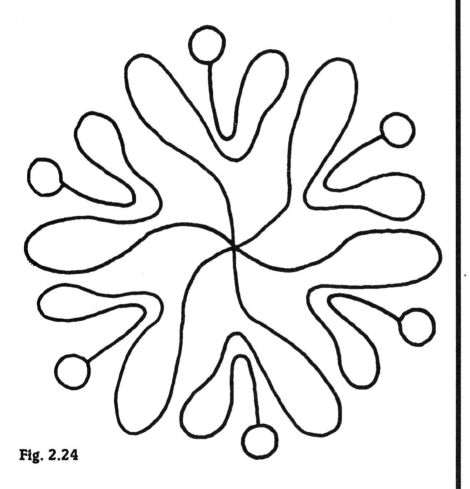

Fig. 2.24

Fig. 2.24 Trace this flower design for the rug.

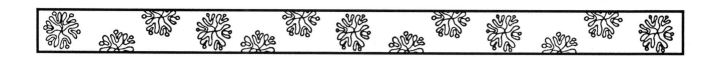

Rug size: 21" X 36" (53.3cm X .9m)

Stitch width: 3

Stitch length: 1 – 2

Needle: #90/14 jeans

Thread: top, monofilament, bobbin, red and monofilament

Presser foot: open embroidery foot

Fabric: purchased woven rug

Yarn: pink, bright rose, dark rose, light sage, dark sage, yellow cotton Sugar 'n Cream

Miscellaneous: fine crochet hook or darning needle, tracing paper, marker, washable fabric glue

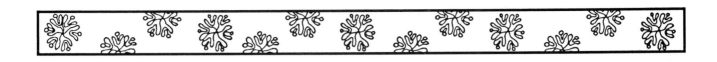

Once I had a design on paper (Fig. 2.24), I made many more copies of it (I used 14). If you don't have access to a copier, then trace them out of the book, using tracing paper and a marker. Cut around the outside edges of the motifs to make paper circles.

Place the rug on the floor, underside up; arrange and rearrange the paper circles until you decide their placement. Decision made, pin the circles to the rug. Then stitch the circles down, monofilament on the top, red thread in the bobbin.

Once the designs are transferred, clip several 6" (15.2cm) lengths of yarn from each of the balls of yarn and drop them onto the flower circles, moving them around until the color arrangement is pleasing. Pin the yarn to the designs on the rug for future color reference as you stitch.

Each design is made up of three separate sections. Complete each section in one pass with one length of yarn. You'll need three strands, each 24" (61cm) for each motif.

Poke the end of the first piece of yarn to the back (at a point under the top loop of the flower, leaving about 1/2" (1.5cm) as a tail. Use either the darning needle or pull it through with a crochet hook. Zigzag (stitch width 3, stitch length 1-1/2) over the yarn, following the red stitching lines (Fig. 2.25). Use the open embroidery foot (Fig. 2.26) rather than a cording or appliqué foot, because you'll have more control turning sharp curves with the yarn. Finish the pass, poke the yarn through to the back and cut it off 1/2" (1.5cm) from the rug. Continue stitching down the other pieces of yarn. If the rug gets in your way as you stitch, roll it up and pin it, leaving open only the area you're stitching. Continue stitching in all the designs.

Tear off any paper patterns from the back that haven't fallen off already. Clip off any thread ends, then glue down the short ends of yarn underneath with washable glue. Isn't it easy to create an original?

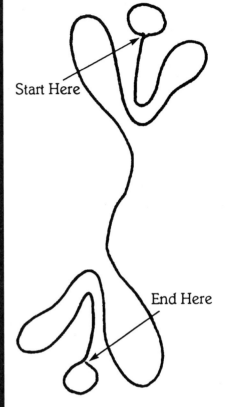

Start Here

End Here

Fig. 2.25

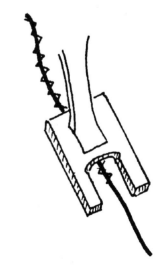

Fig. 2.26

Fig. 2.25 Start and stop stitching at these points

Fig. 2.26 Use the open embroidery foot for better visibility when couching yarn.

Chapter II **Appliquéd and Embroidered 31**

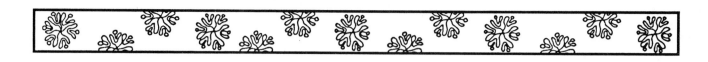

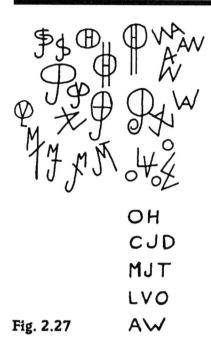

OH
CJD
MJT
LVO
AW

Fig. 2.27

More Cheater Rug ideas: Of course you don't have to *sew* on these rugs to decorate them. You can stencil them or dip foam rubber designs into fabric paints and stamp them. (Dip and print is a project young children can understand and do for gifts or for their own rooms. And don't they all have enough painted T-shirts by now?) One of my favorite sponges is available at craft stores. It is a thinly compressed cellulose sponge. After cutting out a pattern, you soak the sponge in water and it expands. Then it's ready to print.

But let's get back to sewing: To make the rug gift both original and personal, try my favorite quick-rug gift idea using a commercially woven rug. First write down the initials of the friend who'll receive the rug and then simplify the letters—shorten or lengthen them, combine or overlap all three or only one or two of them. The fun is in not making the monograms look like monograms—you want them to look like interesting line designs. It's only on second glance that the letters become obvious.

After deciding on a design, make a dozen or so copies of it and proceed as I did with the Cheater's Rug, choosing colors you know they can use in a kitchen, a hallway, or by a back door. (Yes, you can stamp the monograms on, too, if you are the type who finishes up gifts five minutes before the party.)

Fig. 2.27 Make monograms into personal designs for rugs.

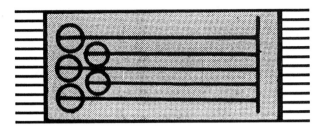

Fig. 2.28

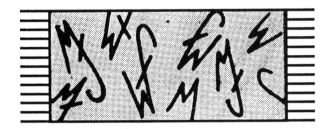

Fig. 2.29

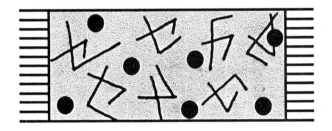

Fig. 2.30

Fig. 2.27 Using the initials OT (or DCL?) a rug design is born.

Fig. 2.29 Another example of a monogram (MJT) design.

Fig. 2.30 LVO is easy to use.

Chapter II **Appliquéd and Embroidered 33**

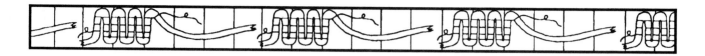

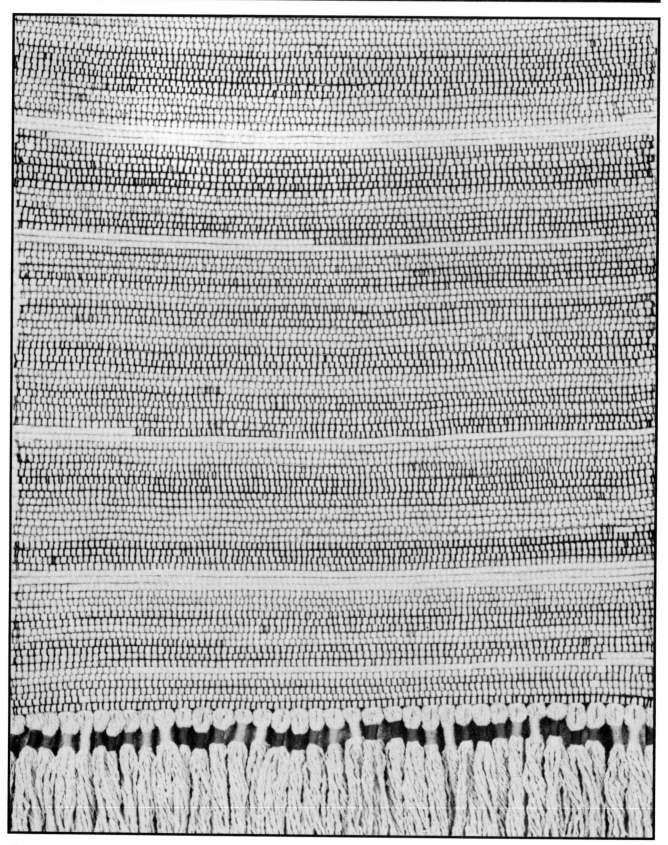

4. Buttonhole and Rope Rug

This small rug is especially fitting in a country-style home. It looks like a woven rug, but all you need to make it is a "buttonhole" stitch (Fig. 2.31) on your sewing machine.

Rug size: 22" X 32" (56cm X 81cm)

Stitch width: 0 – 6

Stitch length: 2 – 4

Needle: #120/20 jeans

Thread: top, white polyester, cordonnet (Metrosene) in a dozen earth-tone colors; bobbin, white polyester

Presser foot: general purpose

Fabric: two pieces 24" X 34" (61cm X 86.5cm) heavy canvas for backings

Rope: 300 ft. (91.5m) or 6 hanks sash cord (solid, braided cotton—buy at a hardware store); twisted, cotton roping for 72 (9" (23cm) tassels (buy at weaver's store or see Sources of Supplies)

Miscellaneous: 6" X 24" (15cm X 61cm) ruler and permanent marker, tassel maker (see Sources of Supplies) or 9" (23cm) piece of cardboard, small screwdriver, several long quilter's pins, hand-sewing needle, washable fabric glue (e.g., Glu N' Wash); two strips of 1"-wide (2.5cm) fusible webbing 24" (61cm) long and 2 strips, 34" (86.5cm) long; clip clothespins

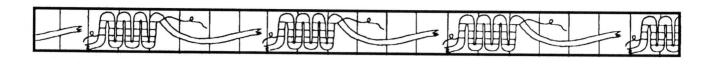

Fig. 2.31

Sash cord is sewn to a backing (which doesn't show) by couching over the cord with a stitch that mimics a handmade buttonhole stitch. Use a braided cord because roping untwists, grows fatter, and is more impossible to cover.

Use Method 1 in Appendix A to finish the backing, then mark stitching guide lines across it the short way, using the ruler and permanent marker. I marked every 2" (5cm).

Choose a cord with a diameter less than the widest stitch your machine will allow. The diameter of the cord I used was 4.76mm and my machine buttonhole stitch is 6mm, so this is a good choice. As I stitched, I found that one hank (50 ft. or 15m) covered 6" (15cm) of my rug, so I needed 6 hanks of cord for my 36" (.9m) rug. Whatever you choose, use a cord or yarn that doesn't flatten completely as you sew over it. The braid I chose has a core and is extremely stiff.

To choose stitch length, elongate the buttonhole stitch until it looks like carpet warp over the rope. The presser foot rides on top of the ropes as the needle stitches into the backing on both the right and left swings.

As you sew the cord down, change cordonnet colors many times—usually in the middle of a row.

To begin, start at the left-hand edge of the canvas. Leave a 3" (7.5cm) tail of cord, then set the machine on the "buttonhole" (see page 23, Fig. 2.19) settings chosen and stitch down the length of the first row. At the end, turn the cord and stitch in the other direction. Leave a short loop at the edge beyond the backing fabric. The edges tend to be the most difficult area to hold the two cords next to each other. Use the small screw driver that came with your machine to push the cord up, next to the previous row. If the cord still curves slightly in the middle, as mine did, you can stitch cords slightly apart in the middle of the row to even up the braid as you progress (Fig. 2.32), and there's also a way to fix the braids when the rug is finished, which I'll show you how to do later.

Fig. 2.31 Couch down cord with stitch that imitates hand-sewn buttonhole stitch.

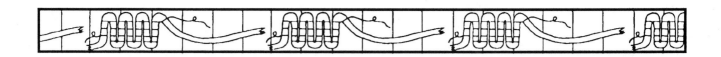

When joining cords in the middle of the rug (never start a new cord at the edge!) cut the two cords on a slant, dab the ends with glue stick, then butt them up next to each other and stitch over them (Fig. 2.33). I used pins, too, to help keep the cords together as I stitched over them. The join is practically invisible.

When the rug is finished, leave a 3" (7.5cm) tail as you did at first.

Measure the rug to get the exact dimensions. Fold under the second piece of heavy canvas fabric to fit the rug dimension. Slip in and press a 1" (2.5cm) strip of fusible webbing at all four sides. Then fold each edge back toward the center and press as in Method 1 in Appendix A.

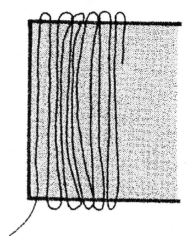

Fig. 2.32

Pull rug into shape and pin the back of the rug to the canvas. Slip the ends of the ropes (at the beginning and end) inside between the two pieces of canvas. Stitch the backings together by straight stitching between the ropes with white polyester thread. First stitch down the center, then straight stitch down at each end inside the last row of rope. Go back and stitch every 2" (5cm) or 3" (7.5cm). Pull the rows of cords straight as you attach the two backings. This evens up the rows.

For the next step, use Glu N' Wash glue or any other type that can be laundered and remains flexible. Squirt small dots of glue between back and inside rug at each long edge. Line canvas edges up to the backing edges and press in place. Use clip clothespins to keep the edges together until the glue is dry.

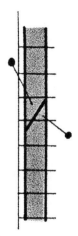

Fig. 2.33

Make 9" (23cm) long tassels for the short ends using household string, roping, or cord to match the sash cord (don't use the braid). Wrap the top of each tassel by hand with the threads used for buttonhole stitching or choose cotton yarn in the same colors. (See Rug 1, Figs. 2.8 and 2.9.) Hand stitch them to the rug with polyester thread, catching the backing and lining.

Fig. 2.32 If the cord bows when attaching it, gradually straighten it on subsequent rows.

Fig. 2.33 To join two cords, cut cords on slants; glue, pin, then stitch over the cord.

Chapter II **Appliquéd and Embroidered 37**

Raveled, Fringed, and Looped

- **Plaid Ravel Rug**
- **Yarn and Fringe Fork Rug**
- **Fabric and Fringe Fork Rug**
- **T-shirts and Fringe Fork Rug**
- **Instant Rug**
- **Confetti Pompom Rug**
- **Upholstery Fringed Rug**
- **Fringed Linen Rug**

III. Raveled, Fringed, and Looped

No machine-made rug book is complete without the traditional fringe-fork rugs, but once I wrapped and stitched down the obligatory rug yarn, I went on to make samples using different types and lengths of yarn, leaving the loops clipped or unclipped. I discovered that all fringe-fork rugs don't have to look the same.

My favorite yarn was made from narrow strips of T-shirt fabric that were pulled into tubes. Once wrapped around the fringe fork, sewn into place and clipped, the curled tubes of cotton knit stood up from the backing like perfect flower centers. It was a look I hadn't expected, but so exciting I knew this sample would definitely be one of the rugs included in the book.

Another experiment that went right was when I wondered how many ways I could change the surface of a plain stencil rug. Soon I ran out of rugs, but never ran out of ideas: Add fringe or strips of fabric to rugs; couch down yarn to mimic rugs from India or use crewel designs from Early American embroidery; experiment with appliques. One of my ideas, the Instant Rug, is included here.

Another one of the rugs you can make (Upholstery Fringed Rug) is ready-made, too, but you prepare the backing, then stitch purchased fringes to it.

A favorite of mine is the Plaid Ravel Rug, which uses unraveled sweaters. I find the use of old wool-knit sweaters instead of new yarn so inventive. The rug is easily stitched together, and exactness and neatness don't count (no one can tell).

Not only is there an overlapping of methods in many of these rugs, but I discovered that different methods often result in the same look. The Confetti Pompom Rug looks like the Yarn and Fringe Fork Rug. The rug made with strips of fabric wound on the fringe fork resembles the Amish Doubleknit Dust Catcher or the Carmen Miranda rug found in Chapter 5. After making samples, you can decide which method you like best.

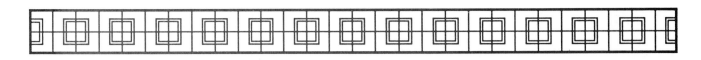

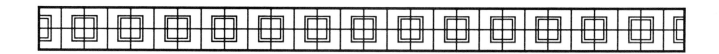

5. Plaid Ravel Rug

It's impossible to tell how this rug is made or of what it's made if you don't know about ravel rugs. They're believed to be Shaker in origin, although this has never been proved. But the nineteenth-century Shakers were involved in the knitted underwear business, and what better source for the knitted scraps needed for this rug? Wool knitted mittens and socks also were used, but I'd never found any detailed directions until I found reference to a ravel mat in a 1928 magazine.

Instead of using strips already knitted, the rug maker was directed to ravel sweaters, make balls of yarn, then reknit the yarn into long, narrow strips. After steam pressing the strips and stitching them into tubes, they were attached to a backing, then cut apart on the folds and raveled. The next question was—could I survive knitting dozens of boring, long, narrow strips? Not me! I found that step completely unnecessary. My solution to the problem is wool Shetland sweaters. My directions follow:

Rug size: 30" X 42" (76cm X 1m)

Stitch width: 3 – 6

Stitch length: 1-1/2 – 5

Needle: #120/20 jeans

Presser foot: no snag type (see Chapter I)

Thread: top, monofilament; bobbin, white polyester

Fabric: 32" X 42" (.8m X 1m) heavy canvas backing, seven 100 percent wool sweaters cut into strips

Miscellaneous: 6" X 24" (15cm X 61cm) clear plastic ruler; black, red, blue permanent markers; fabric scissors; pointed embroidery scissors (optional); Velcro dots (optional)

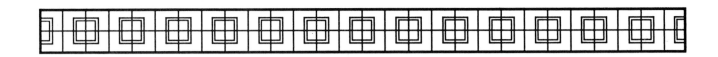

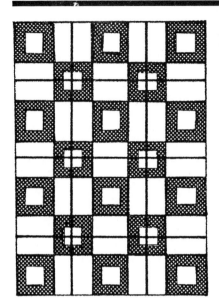

Fig. 3.1

First I found a wool sweater to cut into 1-1/2" (4cm) strips. I didn't steam press it as the sweater was old and I knew it had been pressed dozens of times. From then on I continued following the directions for the 1928 mat. It worked like a charm, so I began collecting wool sweaters.

In our Chicago area, where L. L. Bean and Eddie Bauer are household words, wool Shetland sweaters are uniforms. Thrift shops and garage sales supplied me with all the wool sweaters I'd need for carpeting a house. I paid from 15 cents to $2 per sweater and soon had a collection of 28 navy blue, green, red, and gold woolen sweaters. I had no idea how many I'd need, so I kept collecting. When choosing sweaters, I kept in mind that tightly knitted sweaters produce tightly curled ravelings; worsted weight ravelings, as found in Shetlands, are looser, but an excellent, curly surface evolves as you ravel back on it; and extremely loose, bulky knits don't work well.

It's important to use 100 percent wool because the kink, pressed in when wool sweaters are blocked, stays curled. Cottons or acrylics and other man-made yarns lose their curliness.

Fig. 3.1 Ravel rug pattern: Stitch two rows of green tubes around each 6" (15cm) square, two rows of gold down and across on intersecting lines, dark blue in 6" (15cm) and 4" (10cm) white squares, dark red in shaded areas.

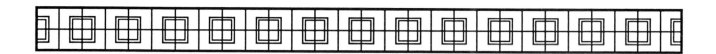

Although I planned a plaid rug (Fig. 3.1) because I thought stitching knit tubes down in straight lines is easier than stitching in circles, I found out later it's possible to stitch more complicated designs. Remember, though, the edges won't be defined exactly; I think that's the charm of this rug.

Cut off the sleeves and remove the neck ribbing from your sweaters. You may cut off the ribbing on the sleeves and sweater body, too, if they are so tight they pull the strips out of shape. Otherwise, leave them in place. Cut off any buttons and plackets and cut side seams off the body and sleeves. Open the sleeves and place one sleeve over the other to cut the sleeves into 1-1/2" (4cm) wide strips from top to bottom (Fig. 3.2). If you are cutting with a scissors, follow the groove between knitted stitches—it's an easy guide. If using a rotary cutter, it's not necessary to follow the groove exactly. In other words, don't slow yourself down by searching for the groove and trying to keep the ruler in place. Once it's raveled it won't show. Cut the body of the sweater in the same way.

Remember: Always cut the sweater by cutting *between* stitches, not across the rows. Otherwise, when you come to ravel the tubes, your stitches will disappear as they do when you're raveling out a knitting mistake.

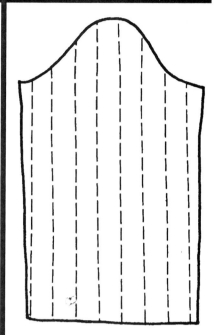

Fig. 3.2

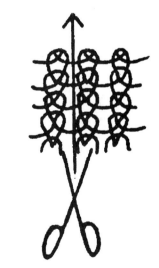

Fig. 3.3

Fig. 3.2 Cut knit strips in this direction.

Fig. 3.3 Cut knitting from bottom to top, not across the bodice or sleeve.

Chapter III **Raveled, Fringed, and Looped** **43**

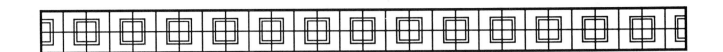

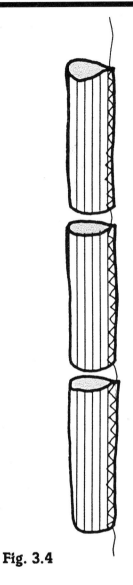

Fig. 3.4

To make knit tubes, fold each strip in half the long way and zigzag or serge the cut edges together (stitch width 3, stitch length 1-1/2). Since you will unravel them eventually, it doesn't matter whether you put wrong or right sides together (Fig. 3.4). Stitch one after another, never bothering to anchor thread as you create one long string of knit tubes. I didn't know how many sweaters I'd need, so I began by stitching tubes from one gold, two green, two red and three blue sweaters. Altogether, I probably needed fewer than seven sweaters, but again, because the rug is a plaid, this is an estimate. I did have some tubes left over in each color—some more than others.

With the ruler and permanent markers in red, blue and black, draw the plaid on the top of the backing. Use different markers to indicate color changes.

In my collection of 28 sweaters, there were few that were the same colors or the same size knit, although all of them were 100 percent wool. As I stitched the tubes in place, I combined three or four different navy blues into one square, and followed the same procedure with the dark red. It's not necessary to draw in each stitching line, but stitch one tube as closely as you can to the next (stitch width 6, stitch length 1-1/2). The presser foot keeps it at least 1/4" (6mm) from the one before. This keeps the tubes standing up. When raveled, you can leave several knit stitches where the tube is attached to ensure the yarn is not pulled out in wear (Fig. 3.5B).

When stitching the plaid rug, I followed this sequence: first I stitched in the gold grids, two tubes wide. Next came the green outlines around each square. Those are also two tubes wide. To save time, I cut several blue and red tubes into lengths that fit the squares; then I could apply and stitch one after another without stopping. I filled one square at a time. Surprisingly, this was not a difficult rug to manipulate, but if you want to make a larger ravel rug, prepare several small ones and sew them together later.

Why do you have to go through all the trouble of stitching strips into tubes when you can zigzag the strip down the center, attaching it to the canvas at the same time? I'll tell you why I don't do it that way. It's easier to manipulate and stitch down tubes. I can cut on the fold, thus dividing the strip

Fig. 3.4 Stitch tubes together, one after another.

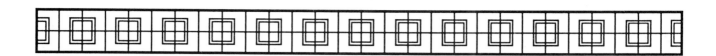

exactly in half. And it's stitched exactly where I want it. If the strip is stitched down the center, sometimes it is not stitched straight on the backing, and often it is not stitched exactly in the center of the strip.

I discovered that direction makes no difference when stitching down the tubes. In other words, they can be placed next to each other, or around in a circle. You'll never be able to tell once the tubes are raveled.

Fig. 3.5A

After the tubes are in place, cut through the folds (Fig. 3.5A). If you're a knitter, you know that raveling a sweater from the top down is fast. Raveling from the bottom up is not. The same is true with tubed strips. Once you've slit through the fold, begin raveling "from the top." To discover which end is the top, pull the knit stitches to one side at the edge. If they fringe away from the rest of the strip without difficulty, then continue fringing. If not, then try the other end. Use a closed, short, pointed scissors to nudge loops apart. Ravel to one or two stitches from the zigzagging (Fig. 3.5B). You may be able to ravel the stitches without the use of the scissors if the knitting is loose.

Fig. 3.5B

If you can't wait for Shetland sweaters to wear out, or if you can't find the colors you want, but you don't want to hand knit strips, there is one more alternative—knitting by machine. I admit, I used the colors I found most often in Shetland sweaters and used Shetlands because they are 100 percent wool, but you may not want to be limited by the sweaters you find. Borrow or invest in a simple knitting frame. Inexpensive, the cost of one is less than what you'd pay for a rug like this in a store.

The rug can be left as raveled, but to protect the stitches on the backing, and also to hide them, I suggest you make a second backing. See Method 1 in Appendix A for how to finish the rug. Then attach dots of Velcro on top and to the backing to temporarily hold the backing to the rug while it's being used.

Country decorators will find this rug an interesting conversation piece.

Fig. 3.5
   A. Cut tube through fold.
   B. Leave several knit stitches unraveled at the bottom of each tube.

Chapter III **Raveled, Fringed, and Looped** **45**

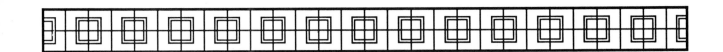

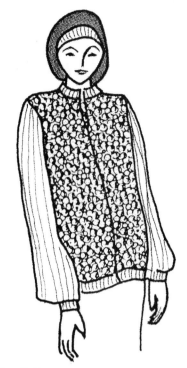

Fig. 3.6

Fig. 3.7

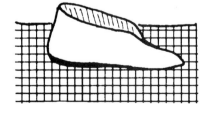

Fig. 3.8

More ravel ideas: Have you seen quilted or fur jackets with knitted sleeves? Or pull-overs using quilting and sweatshirt fleece sleeves? Use a commercial pattern and the ravel rug technique to duplicate either one of these ideas. Instead of canvas, use a poplin-weight fabric for the backing of the body, to cut down on weight and bulk (you may also want to cut narrower tubes for the same reason). Then knit sleeves to match (or look through your sweaters before you cut them in strips—can you find an acceptable sweater with useable sleeves?). Knit ribbing for the bottom of the garment (do you think you can find a sweater with both sleeves and ribbing?) and add ribbing around the neckline, too.

Another idea presented itself when I took a class from my friend, Margaret Bowman. Margaret created clever boots (they've been featured in exhibits, magazines, and art-to-wear books), which she quilted, Seminole pieced, embroidered—or all three on one pair.

Fig. 3.6 This ravel jacket has knitted sleeves.

Fig. 3.7 Margaret Bowman's ravel boots for cold winter nights.

Fig. 3.8 Place a fabric slipper on graph paper to make your own pattern.

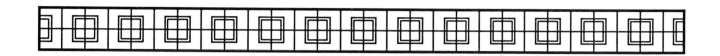

Everyone in our boot class first made a personal boot pattern. The legs of the boots reached to the knee and we could embellish them any way we wished. You guessed it: my boots (warm footwear for cold evenings) are raveled sweaters.

Even if you aren't lucky enough to have taken Margaret's class, you can make your own boots by using a commercial pattern or finding help at the library (see Bibliography). Or you can buy Mukluk soles at knit shops and use the raveled sweaters instead of knitting the sock part. Of course, if you have a pair of fabric slippers that fit you, then use them for a pattern, tracing the sole on graph paper and using a ruler and graph paper to measure and record all the slipper pieces. Cut the pattern from the paper and start fringing.

Two of Margaret's hints: use "Safe Treds" (a rubber-like gripper fabric for the soles—it's found on the soles of children's sleepers) and on the inside place a fleece or terry innersole (available at variety and drug stores).

Fig. 3.9

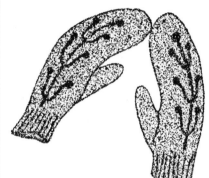

Fig. 3.10

Fig. 3.9 and Fig. 3.10 Make a ravel cap and mits for a blustery day.

Chapter III **Raveled, Fringed, and Looped** **47**

6. Yarn and Fringe Fork Rug

The Confetti Pompom Rug and this rug made with a fringe fork can result in the same look. Or, if you make the fringe short and unclipped, the surface resembles rug hooking.

Rug size: 22" X 40" (56cm x 1m)

Stitch width: 3 – 5

Stitch length: 1 – 1/2

Needle: #90/14 jeans

Thread: top, monofilament; bobbin, white polyester

Presser Foot: no snag type (see Chapter I)

Fabric: heavy canvas or striped pillow ticking backing

Yarn: polyester rug yarn (determine amount by doing a sample. I used 14 skeins (each 60 yards (54m), 3 ply): 4 white, 4 light blue, 6 dark blue

Accessories: 1-3/4" (4cm) wide fringe fork, 6" X 24" (15cm X 61cm) clear plastic ruler, permanent marker, adding machine tape

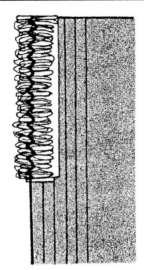

Fig. 3.11

Use Method 1 in Appendix A to finish the rug, but leave one long side unfinished until you are within one skein of completion so you can tell exactly where the right edge should be. The exact size of this rug is never known until you've finished stitching as it has too many variables. I can only hope that when you begin with a rug the length I used, with a fringe fork the size I used, and wrap the fork as tightly and push down the loops as closely as I did, one skein of yarn will fill two rows plus a few inches (centimeters) of a third row—but I know that no two rugs are ever alike. Even if I did this rug over again, it would not be exactly the same as the first.

Be sure to stitch a sample first to determine how close together the lines of fringe should be placed. If the edge rolls tightly underneath, stitch rows farther apart. If only a slight roll, which this type of rug wants to do, proceed stitching the rug, then place a second backing on the rug when it's finished (see Appendix A).

Once you've determined the distance between rows, use the marker and ruler to draw stitching lines down the length of the backing or mark which rows to stitch on if striped pillow ticking is used.

Fig. 3.11 When stitching down the center, attach to adding machine tape first, then to backing.

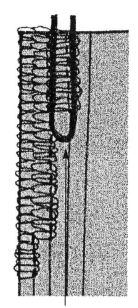

When using the fringe fork, you have a choice of stitching down the middle of the yarn, or to one side. I usually prefer the middle because I can cover more space in less time. I use Robbie Fanning's method and stitch the yarn to strips of adding machine tape first (stitch width 3, stitch length 1-1/2) before I apply it to the fabric backing (Fig. 3.11). The strips don't twist, and I have more control over colors and space when applying them to the backing later. Always stitch down the exact center of the fringe or the loops won't be even.

If you prefer stitching the yarn fringes directly to the backing, then use the other method: stitch along the right side of the fringe fork (Fig. 3.12). It is much easier to apply the fringe strips in a straight line, and keep fringes from the previous row held out of the way.

For this rug, I first stitched up fringe on adding machine tape long enough to accommodate one skein apiece. This helped me determine later how much fringe to apply to the backing at one time (each different color section on the rug is one skein). I stitched fringe from two skeins of white yarn, two of light blue, but three skeins of dark blue. When finished, I stitched combinations of yarns by wrapping two colors together: one skein each of white/light blue, white/dark blue and light blue/dark blue. I folded the combination strips in half and cut them in two pieces (each is then one skein).

Pull Out

Fig. 3.12

Fig. 3.12 When stitching loops directly to the backing, stitch at the side of the fork.

Chapter III **Raveled, Fringed, and Looped** **51**

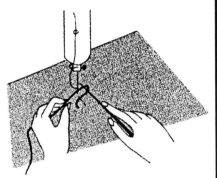

Fig. 3.13

To stitch the fringe to the rug, I started at the left-hand side of the backing so the bulk of the rug is always to the left of the needle. Before I started stitching the first skein of dark blue fringe to the backing, I folded the adding machine tape under and to the right of the fringe. Then I placed the center of the fringe over the edge of the backing and zigzagged it in place (stitch width 5, stitch length 1-1/2). When stitching was completed, I tore off the adding machine tape from that row of fringe. All subsequent rows of fringe were stitched down on the marked lines, following the previous directions.

After the dark blue rows, I added one half of the light blue/dark blue combination I prepared, starting exactly where the dark blue ended on the third line.

After that was stitched in place, I added a skein of light blue fringe.

Next, I stitched down one strip of the light blue/white combination, then went on with a skein of white fringe, one strip of the white/dark blue fringe, ending in the center of the backing with a skein of dark blue.

The second half of the rug is a mirror image of the first: white/dark blue, white, light blue/white, light blue, dark blue/light blue, ending with a skein of dark blue at the right edge.

Fig. 3.13 With or without a presser foot, stitch loops individually to add patches of color.

Above: *Wrapped and coiled craft cord is zigzagged to make an oval rug.*

Rugs in this color section:

Coiled Craft Cord

Quilted Bath Mat

Flat Folds and Clipped Strips Chair

Denim Chenille

Fabric and Fringe Fork

Fringed Linen

Buttonhole and Rope

Caterpillar

Cheater's

Plaid Ravel

Above: Buy extra towels to make a matching bath mat.

Right: Use this clipped strips technique to make chair pads.

Far Right: Denim strips are stitched so closely together on the chenille mat that they stand on edge.

Machine-Made Rugs

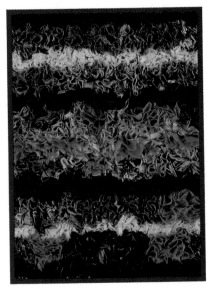

Above: Construct this rug by wrapping fabric strips around a fringe fork.

Machine-Made Rugs

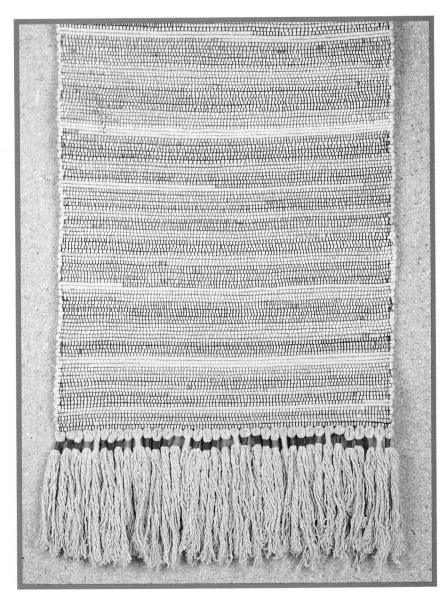

Above: *Fringe layers of loosely woven fabric strips for this accent rug.*

Above: *Buttonhole stitches over rope imitate handweaving.*

Machine-Made Rugs

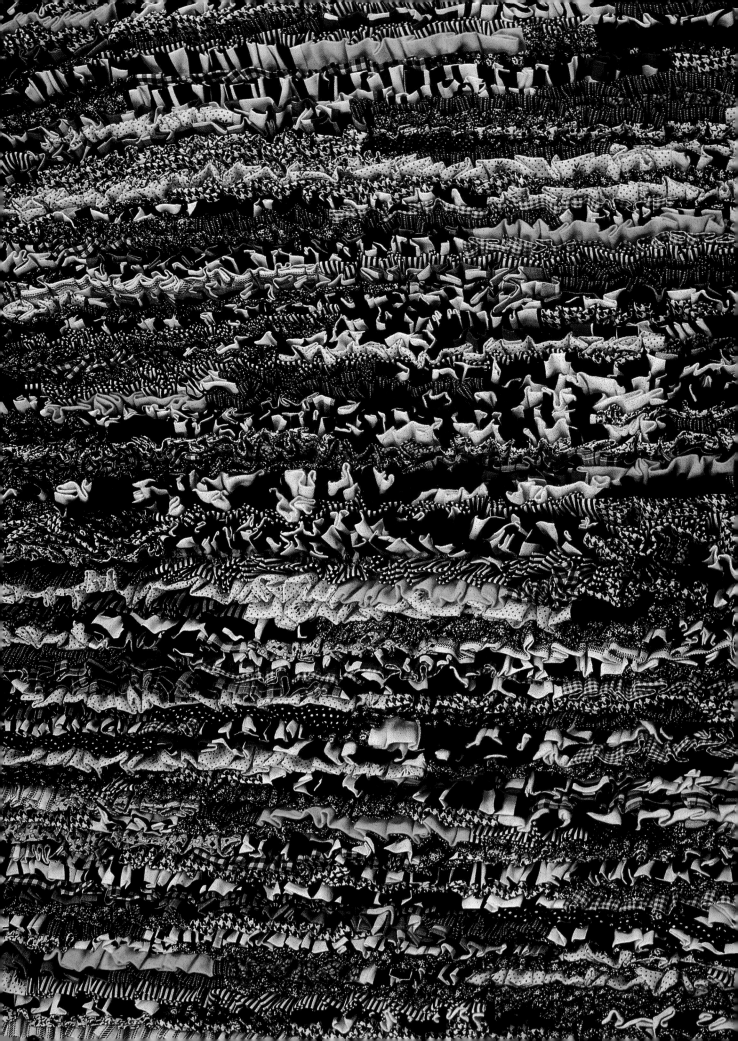

Above: Embellish purchased woven rugs to make the Cheater's Rug.

Left: This rug is made from gathered tubes of fabric called caterpillars.

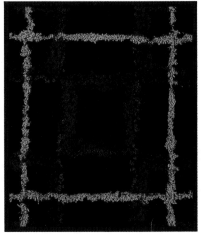

Above: *Raveled wool Shetland sweaters create texture for this rug.*

Machine-Made Rugs

Before I stitched down the dark blue fringe, I had to finish the edge. I measured the backing I'd need to finish the rug—I needed at least two rows for one skein of yarn—and added 1" (2.5cm) to fold over and stitch in place. When that was accomplished, I finished the rug by stitching down the rows of dark blue fringe (you may have a piece left over).

I placed the rug on a flat surface and clipped through the center of each loop.

Next, I used the tassel maker (or you can cut a piece of cardboard 6" (15cm) long) to wrap dark blue yarn into clumps of fringe. Each was wrapped ten times, then tied off at the top with another piece of yarn and cut from the tassel tool at the other end. Each of these pieces of fringe was tacked by hand 1" (2.5cm) apart at each end of the rug to finish it.

To add designs such as flowers or leaves or small patches of color, it is easier to forego the fringe fork. Instead, stitch loops in, one at a time (Fig. 3.13). Begin by stitching ends of colored yarn to the backing, then lifting loops with a knitting needle or skewer, stitching the loops in place, lifting another, and so on, until the area is filled.

More yarn fringe ideas: As with ravel rugs, you can take yarn fringe out of the realm of rugs and use it for clothing embellishment (uncut, short loops make an attractive addition to the cuffs and neckline of a sweater—Fig. 3.14), add it to curtains, use it for pillows, make a teddy bear, or make super-wide yards of it for a lion's mane on Halloween.

Fig. 3.14

Fig. 3.14 Yarn loops the neckline and cuffs of a knitted sweater.

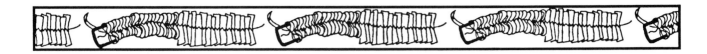

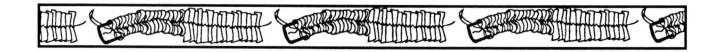

7. Fabric and Fringe Fork Rug

Want to get rid of outdated fabric, fabric you dislike, or scraps that look too small for any use? This rug is the answer. Once it's finished, you won't recognize flowers, plaids, or stripes because all you'll see are blended colors.

Rug size: 23-1/2" X 37-1/2" (60cm x 96cm)

Stitch width: 3

Stitch length: 1-1/2

Needle: #100/16 jeans

Thread: top, monofilament; bobbin, white polyester

Presser foot: no snag type (see Chapter I)

Fabric: use scraps at least 1" (2.5cm) wide (strips cut on the straight or bias). I used approximately 11 yards (9.9m) 24" X 36" (61cm X .9m) heavy canvas or striped pillow ticking backing

Miscellaneous: 6" X 24" (15cm X 61cm) clear plastic ruler, rotary cutter and mat, permanent marker, 2-1/4" (6cm) fringe fork; adding machine tape

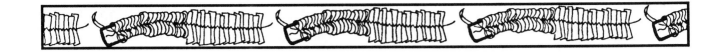

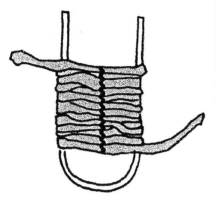

Fig. 3.15

This rug is made with a fringe fork, but the results can resemble the Amish Doubleknit Dust Catcher (see Chapter 5) if the fabric strips are overlapped neatly and evenly spaced on the fringe fork. For a completely different, Carmen Miranda look, wrap the fork while on the machine, pushing the loops quite close together. That is the look I chose for the rug pictured. I stitched with machine settings at stitch width 1-1/2, stitch length 1-1/2. This is a close zigzag, but it insures I anchor all the pleats and folds tightly. They're those same pleats and folds that make the loops and fringes stand up straight from the backing later.

Prepare the backing using Method 1 from Appendix A. If you use canvas, mark it in lines 1/2" (1.5cm) apart with the ruler and marker, or use stripes of ticking as a guide.

Cut these strips 1" wide (1.5cm) on the straight, even though bias strips ravel less. Strips cut on the grain are stronger—especially when they are this narrow. (Try a sample of both to see which you like best. Wash and dry both of them to see which one you'll like best in the future.)

Cut many strips at once using the rotary cutter and mat. Short strips, long strips, it makes no difference. Even if you have uneven scraps of fabric, cut them up to use what you can. Although some of my rows of fringe are scraps of many colors, I planned to use dark brown, white, and pink rows to make the rug look planned rather than scrap-like (I also had many yards of those colors in my collection and wanted to use them up). I estimated I'd need 10 yards (9m), and came close to that, but you can cut fabric as you need it if you don't want to overestimate.

Fig. 3.15 Without removing the fringe fork from the machine, carelessly overlap and push strips together (they'll automatically pleat and fold) for a Carmen Miranda look.

Count the number of stitching lines you've drawn on the rug backing and cut that same number of adding machine tape strips, the same length as the stitching lines.

Wrap the fringe fork with one of the fabric strips and place it at one end of a piece of adding machine tape. How close the wraps are depends on the look you want. Pushing the wraps close, or wrapping two strips at a time, creates a thick texture. Zigzag in place (see Yarn and Fringe Fork Rug, page 49).

When all the fabric fringe is made, apply the strips to the backing by folding the edge of the paper under and to the right of the fringe. Place the center of the fringe on top of the left edge of the backing and zigzag (stitch width 3, stitch length 1-1/2) down the center of the fabric fringe to the end of the tape. Tear off the adding machine tape. Keep stitching rows of fringe across the rug until finished (Fig. 3.17).

You may want to go back and and clip the loops. If the rows are close enough together, the clipped fringes will stand up, giving the rug an interesting texture.

I had several strips of plain fabric left, so I cut them into 4" long (10cm) pieces and tacked them (by machine zigzag) between rows as shown to give the rug even more texture.

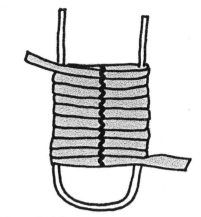

Fig. 3.16

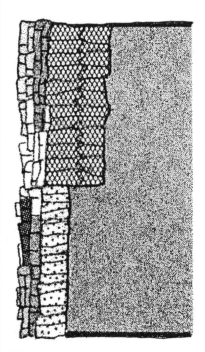

Fig. 3.17

Fig. 3.16 To wrap the fringe fork easily and evenly for an Amish dust catcher look, take the fork off the machine when winding it.

Fig. 3.17 Wrap narrow strips of fabric around a fringe fork and attach to adding machine tape, then to backing and clip.

Chapter III **Raveled, Fringed, and Looped** **57**

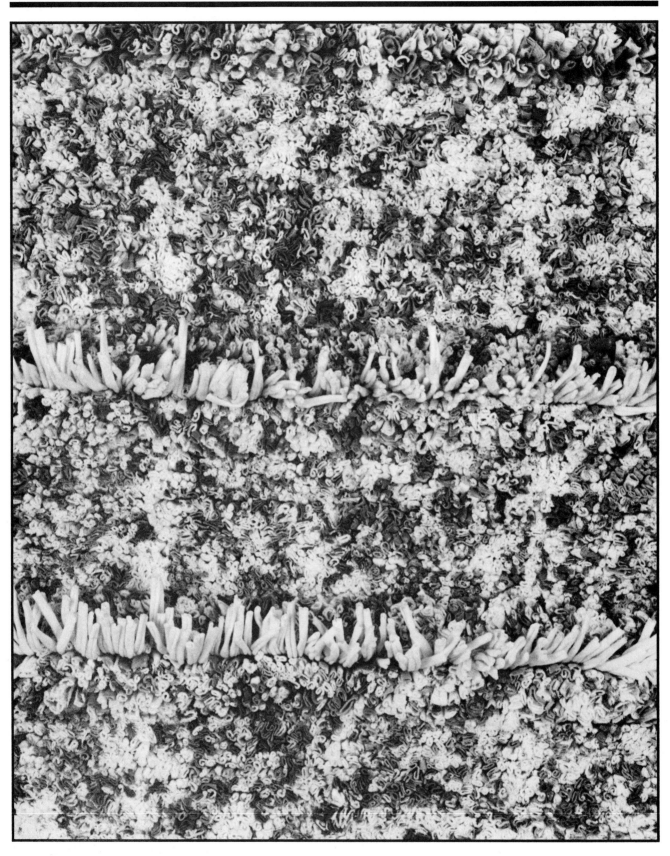

8. T-shirts and Fringe Fork Rug

T his rug could be placed with the Scraps and Strips chapter, except that once T-shirts are cut in narrow strips, then pulled into tubes, the knit fabric behaves and looks more like yarn.

I used several fringe fork sizes and used two types of knit fabric when making this rug. Different fringe lengths and different fabrics create several different textures. The long, white tubes are T-shirt material, but the multi-colored sections are made from T-shirt knit ribbing, which I sprayed with diluted acrylic paints. "Diluted" is the key word. I added three parts water to one part paint because thick paint deters fabric from curling into tubes. Of course you can dye fabrics, too.

Rug size: 20" X 30" (51cm X 76cm)

Stitch width: 0 - 3

Stitch length: 1-1/2

Needle: #100/16

Presser foot: no snag type (see Chapter I)

Fabric: approximately 8-1/2 yards (7.7m) of 45" (1.1m) ribbed T-shirt knit, 2 yards (1.8m) plain T-shirt knit, canvas or pillow ticking for backing (2" (5cm) wider and several inches (centimeters) longer than finished rug size)

Thread: white polyester sewing thread on top and bobbin

Accessories: permanent marker, adding machine tape, appliqué or rug scissors, rotary cutter, mat, and 6" X 24" (15cm X 61cm) clear plastic ruler, three fringe forks: 1-3/4" (4.5cm), 3-1/2" (9cm), 4" (10cm), acrylic paints, spray bottle

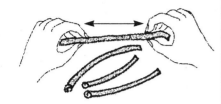

Fig. 3.18

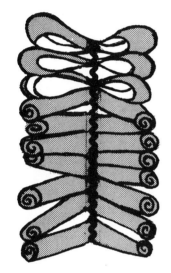

Fig. 3.19

Fig. 3.20

Be sure the single-knit T-shirt fabric you use will curl into tubes. To do this, test the fabric first by pulling at a cut edge. Does it curl? Then it's acceptable. How much fabric you need is determined by how long the fringe is and how closely together it'll be pushed together on the fork as well as the space between stitching lines.

If you paint your fabric instead of using colored T-shirts or yardage, the easiest method is to take the fabric outside and place it on the grass or driveway (assuming the drive is clean). Dilute the paints and place the colors in spray bottles (if necessary, you can use one bottle, washing it out each time you change colors as acrylic paints are water-soluble and can be cleaned from the spray bottle easily). Spray over the entire surface of the fabric with each color and leave the fabric outside to dry. (The minute I'd finished spraying, we had a summer rain shower, so I gathered up the fabric and put it into the dryer. It worked just fine. Then I was careful to dry rags and an old rug next in case any paint was still in the dryer—it wasn't.)

Prepare the rug backing using Method 1 from Appendix A, but leave one end unfinished. Begin by marking the first line at least 1" (2.5cm) from the finished end (this allows enough space at the end to sew down the white fringe later). Then mark lines 3/4" (2cm) apart across the backing (if plain canvas is used), or mark the ticking stripes you'll stitch on if

Fig. 3.18 Pull knit strips to make tubes.

Fig. 3.19 Cut loops into fringe.

Fig. 3.20 Make a circular rug by stitching around the outside and up to the center (see Flat Folds and Clipped Strips Chair Rug).

pillow ticking is used. Finish marking lines when you get to a place at least 2" (5cm) from the other end. Then fold back the fabric to allow 1" (2.5cm) of space at the edge, and room to sew on white fringe later. Either glue or stitch the fold-over in place.

Go back and check-mark the lines you'll use for the different fringe fork sizes. I marked this rug by first folding the rug in half the short way to find the center. Then I arbitrarily marked two sections on each side of the center areas of longer fringe I'd stitch down. Each of those areas are three lines wide. (I planned to stitch the long, white fringe down the center of each of those sections on top of the fringe already there).

After the backing is prepared, use the rotary cutter and mat along with the ruler to cut the ribbed T-shirt fabric into 3/4" (2cm) strips, and the white fabric into 1" (2.5cm) strips. Pull at each end simultaneously to curl them into tubes (Fig. 3.18); then treat the tubes as yarn.

Using the painted fabric, wrap the tubes around the fringe fork without stretching the fabric. Place the fringe fork on a strip of adding machine tape. Push the wraps to the end without bunching them tightly, and zigzag stitch down the center of the loops. There is no need to take the fringe fork off the adding machine tape until you've stitched to the end of the tape.

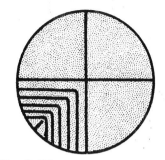

Fig. 3.21

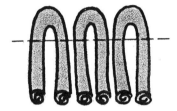

Fig. 3.22

Fig. 3.23

Fig. 3.21 Another way to fill in a circle is to divide it into four parts. Stitch fringe across on the intersecting lines. Add fringe in each section following the lines as shown.

Fig. 3.22 Found on an old rug—rolled strips of flowered rayon folded double and stitched to a sateen backing.

Fig. 3.23 The fabric rolls were arranged in diamond shapes on the backing.

Chapter III **Raveled, Fringed, and Looped** **61**

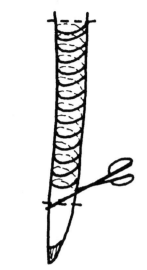

Fig. 3.24

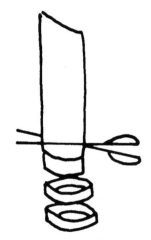

Fig. 3.25

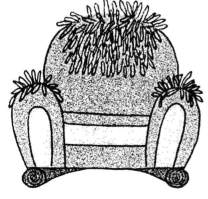

Fig. 3.26

The white fringe is prepared by straight stitching it to the adding machine tape (stitch length 1-1/2). Use the zipper foot to stitch closely at one side of the widest fringe fork. Prepare all your fringes before stitching them to the backing fabric.

When attaching the fringe to the backing, always work from left to right so the bulk of the rug is to the left of the needle at all times. First fold the paper underneath and to the right of the center stitching. Zigzag over the previous stitches as you attach it to the rug backing. As soon as the strip is stitched, tear off the paper. Following your plan, continue adding multi-colored fringes to the lines drawn on the backing.

The white fringe is added last. Cut off most of the adding machine tape to make stitching easier, then place the white fringe down the center on top of the middle rows of long multi-colored fringe and zigzag it in place. Finish by adding white fringe at each end of the rug.

After all the fringe is stitched in place, pull up the center of each loop with a scissors and clip (Fig. 3.19).

Hint: When planning a rug, keep in mind that a wide fringe fork literally eats up fabric. To make your fabric go farther, use a narrower fringe fork and don't bunch up the wraps of fabric as you stitch. Always do a sample first to decide how far apart to stitch the strips.

Fig. 3.24 Cut leg from pantyhose. Starting from one end, cut circularly around the stocking making one long, narrow strip. Stretch into a tube.

Fig. 3.25 Cut leg from pantyhose, then cut across leg into circles 1" (2.5cm) to 2" (5cm) wide. Stretch into tubes.

Fig. 3.26 Instead of crocheted doilies; have fun decorating a chair with fringy T-shirt tubes.

Another hint: Cut adding machine tape the same size as the width of your rug, then count the lines on the backing to determine how many of these strips of tape to cut. Cut all of them before you begin the rug.

To save time later, after cutting out all the adding machine strips I'd need, I counted out twelve strips for the long, painted fringe and put them to one side. Six strips were put in another place for white fringe. The rest of the strips were for short, painted fringe. By doing this ahead of time, I wouldn't waste time counting and recounting strips as I worked.

To keep the texture and density consistent, use the same number of knit tubes for each tape. (After filling one piece of tape and counting the knit strips I used, then counting the lines on the rug backing, I was able to estimate the amount of fabric I needed for the entire rug.)

More T-shirt fringe ideas: Make a vest or a whole jacket (a copy of 1940's fur "chubby"?) or make sweatshirts with fringed yokes or use it as piping in the seams of raglan sleeves. And wouldn't this fringe be perfect for vacation-home decor? Easy-care rugs, of course, but what about coverings for fold-up sling chairs or cushions? It would be unexpected and fun to make antimacassars in wild colors for the backs and arms of over-stuffed chairs.

Remember to try different fringe lengths. What you may reject for one project may look gorgeous on another.

Fig. 3.27

Fig. 3.28

Fig. 3.27 Make a 1940's "chubby" from T-shirt tubes.

Fig. 3.28 Short T-shirt tubes adds pizazz to a sweatshirt seam.

Chapter III **Raveled, Fringed, and Looped** **63**

9. Instant Rug

If there is such a thing as an instant rug, this is it. Buy a woven throw rug, add decoration to it, and it's finished.

Rug size: 24" X 38" (61cm X 96.5cm)

Stitch width: 3

Stitch length: 1-1/2

Needle: #90/14 jeans

Thread: top, monofilament; bobbin, white polyester

Presser foot: no snag (see Chapter I)

Fabric: use a ready-made woven rug (stencil rug— available at craft stores)

Yarn: six balls Sugar 'n' Cream (yellow, light green, dark green, peach, light rose, dark rose)

Miscellaneous: 1-1/4" (3cm) wide fringe fork, adding machine tape

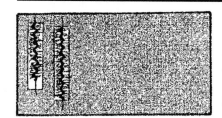

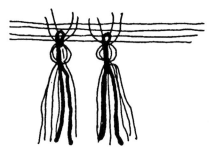

Fig. 3.29

Fig. 3.30

At a craft store, purchase a plain white rug intended for stenciling. Add colored fringes to the rug instead. The yarn used is soft, cotton Sugar 'n' Cream. Begin by cutting six pieces of adding machine tape, each twice as long as the rug is wide (48" or 1.2m).

Wind the fringe fork with yarn, packing it quite closely together to make a thick fringe. Place adding machine tape on the machine, fringe fork over it. Zigzag down the center of the fringe fork (stitch width 3, stitch length 1-1/2). Keep pulling the fork toward you, wrapping and stitching until fringe is completed. Wrap all six colors; then cut each piece in two. Place the rug on the floor and arrange the fringes, cutting some of the strips into smaller lengths. When the arrangement is pleasing to you, pin the strips in place. Don't worry about the adding machine tape. We'll remove it later.

Using the same colors as the fringe you're attaching, place a length of yarn over the center stitching, pinning it in place at both ends. Zigzag over the yarn with the same settings as you used previously (Fig. 3.29). Couching down over a piece of yarn attaches the fringe to the rug and at the same time gives the fringe a cleaner look. It also holds the fringe ends better. When you finish, pull the paper from the stitching and clip all the loops.

Add color to the tassels on the purchased rug if you wish. Thread a darning needle with one of the yarn colors you added to the rug. Draw the yarn up from the bottom, through the tassel knot, over two warp threads at the bottom of the rug, then down through the knot (Fig. 3.30). Clip the ends to meet the end of the tassel. Counting to the right over six threads, I again added the same color to the sixth tassel, then the twelfth. I completed both ends of the rug, then chose another color and added that to the second tassel, the

Fig. 3.29 Attach fringe to rug by stitching over cord.

Fig. 3.30 Add colored cord to tassels.

Fig. 3.31 Try these instant rug ideas:
A. "Buttonhole" over thick cords or yarn.
B. Follow twist of cord to attach it.
C. Stitch down short strips of yarn and fringe ends.

Fig. 3.32 Stack, twist, and stitch down short fabric strips through centers.

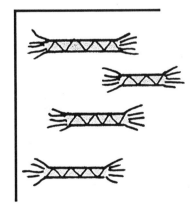

seventh, and so on. All six of the colors were added to the tassels in the same way. Now your rug is finished.

Try other "instant" rugs. Couch down colorful, thick cords by using the "buttonhole" stitch (Fig. 3.31A), or follow the twist of the cord and use monofilament to attach it (Fig. 3.31B). Stitch down short pieces of thick cord or yarn, leaving at least 1/2" (1.5cm) at each end. Fray the ends (Fig. 3.31 C).

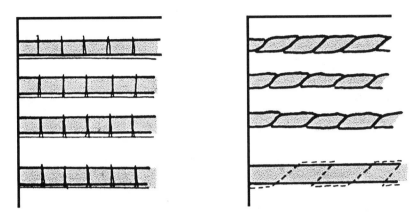

Fig. 3.31A   **Fig. 3.31B**

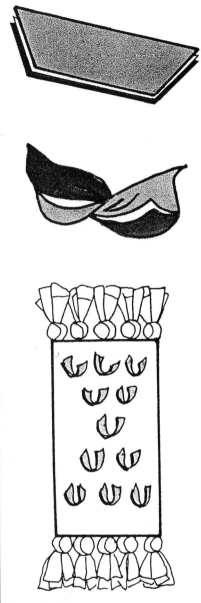

Fig. 3.32

Fig. 3.31C

I saw this "instant" rug in a gallery. Cut three colors of glazed cotton on the bias into 1"-wide (2.5cm) strips. Layer the three colors and cut the strips 3" (7.5cm) long. Twist the strips in the centers and stitch in place with a triple straight stitch, or stitch back and forth through the centers several times. Twist and stitch these wings on the rug in rows or scatter them over the rug (Fig. 3.32).

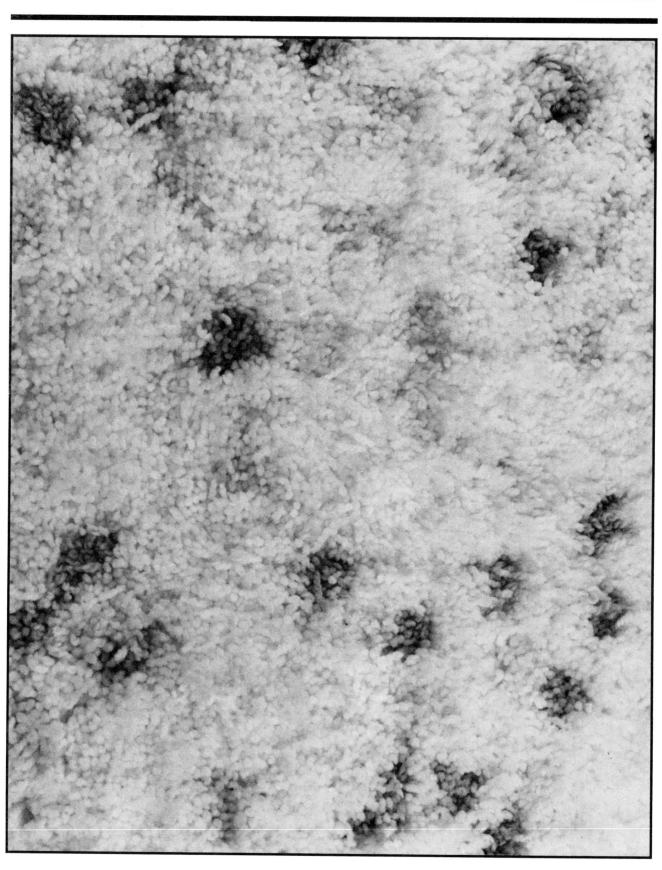

10. Confetti Pompom Rug

The first time my granddaughter bounced onto this pompom rug, she dug her fingers deep into the fuzzy warmth of it and then buried her face in it. It's that kind of rug.

Rug size: 24" X 36" (61cm X .9m)

Stitch width: 3

Stitch length: 1-1/2

Needle: #100/16 jeans

Thread: top, monofilament; bobbin, white polyester

Presser foot: no-snag type (see Chapter I)

Fabric: 26" X 38" (66cm X 96.5cm) canvas backing

Yarn: skeins of Phentex chunky pink, lavender, aqua, yellow, white (This 100 percent acrylic yarn comes in 3 oz. balls, bulky weight, 125 yards (114m) each ball. Make a sample. Number of skeins needed depends on thickness of your yarn)

Miscellaneous: 6" X 24" (15cm X 61cm) clear plastic ruler, marker, rotary cutter and mat, tassel maker or 3" (7.5cm) square piece of cardboard

Note: Now an acceptable Americanization, *pompom* has replaced the French *pompon*, but keeps the original meaning.

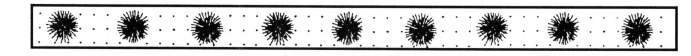

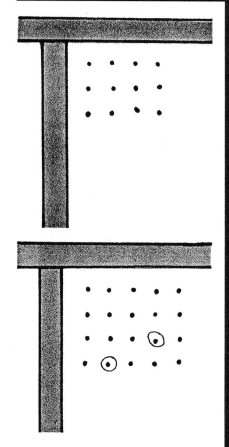

Fig. 3.33

Pompom rugs are usually made by hand. After the pompoms are tied into a bunch, a length of yarn is stitched from the underside of the backing, up and over the pompom, down through the backing again and then tied off. I have several magazines with these directions, but I've never made a pompom that hasn't come apart. Tying it to the backing is never enough to keep the yarn ends from coming loose. Stitching it on the machine is definitely an improvement.

At one time, backings for pompom rugs were sold in needlework shops. Stamped dots (or geometric shapes) were evenly spaced in rows on the backing. I have one with a fish design stamped on it. If I follow the color guide of tiny marks on the backing (dot, triangle, square, circle, etc.), which indicates different colors, I can create an underwater scene with pompoms.

Before I made my rug, I made a 12" (30.5cm) square sample. First I marked dots 1" (2.5cm) apart across and down a piece of canvas (Fig. 3.33). Then I wound 3" (7.5cm) high pompoms (using 6" (15cm) lengths of yarn) with 20 wraps of yarn. After stitching in several rows of pompoms on my canvas (Fig. 3.34), I discovered I had to stitch them farther apart than 1" (2.5cm) or make them skimpier. I knew I was in trouble when the edge began to roll under. How your sample, and eventually your rug, looks depends on four choices: weight (thickness) of yarn, distance between pompoms, number of threads used, and the length of the pompom.

Fig. 3.33 Mark stitching and color guides on backing.

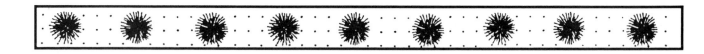

To make stitching easier, use the Elna net curtain foot. If you don't have one, then use a general purpose or embroidery foot. First tape the toes together so you can't catch yarn between them.

You can make most of this rug while sitting comfortably in an easy chair. Use a tassel maker (see Sources of Supplies) to make the job easier. With this tool, any size tassel, up to 6" (15cm), is possible, and there's a slot at the top of the tassel maker to allow you to easily clip through the yarn. Of course you could also cut a piece of heavy cardboard in the size you prefer, then wrap, tie, and cut the pompoms in a uniform length. Remember, as you work, that the tie ends add two more pieces of yarn to the pompom. If you wrap 20 times (40 yarn ends), once tied and cut you add two more ends (42). Keep this in mind when you plan the space.

Use Method 1 or 3 from Appendix A to finish the rug. Mark the rug backing, indicating the correct colors for each pompom. To do this, first mark the backing with black dots the distance apart you prefer (see your sample). As an example, I used 1" (2.5cm) spaces so all the dots are 1" (2.5cm) apart, starting 1" (2.5cm) in from all four sides. Then mark in the confetti colors (around the black dots) that you want to add to the rug.

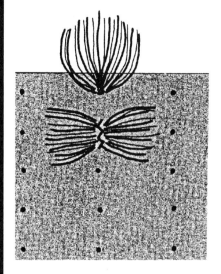

Fig. 3.34

Fig. 3.34 Attach pompoms.

Chapter III **Raveled, Fringed, and Looped** **71**

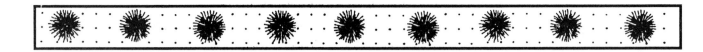

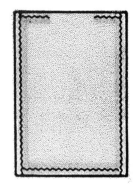

Fig. 3.35

Fig. 3.36

Fig. 3.37

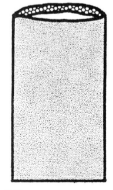

Fig. 3.38

Starting at the left-hand side of the rug, begin stitching on the pompoms. To do this, spread the yarn pompoms apart to find the center, then place the centers over the dots and **zigzag stitch over the center wrap** to attach it to the rug. Follow the color guide as you complete the rug. Working with the bulk of the rug growing to the left is much easier than trying to fit all the pompoms between the machine and needle.

After the pompoms are sewn to the dots, place the rug on a flat surface and clip any pieces of yarn that appear too long. Run your fingers through the rug to bring more to the top. Do this several times across the rug. Don't try to clip it into a perfect surface because that's impossible. But you can clip off those extra-long strands.

Once completed, the pompom rug and the rug made with the yarn-wrapped fringe fork look the same. Only the methods of making the rugs are different, so choose the one you prefer.

By the time you read this, the Confetti Pompom Rug will be a floor pillow for Julie—she asked first.

Years ago I made three floor pillows for our children. They were longer and a great deal wider than the children, and the kids often fell asleep on them in the evenings. I covered them in corduroy and used shredded sponge rubber

Fig. 3.35 Zigzag stitch or serge around the inside pillow case, leaving an area open at one end for turning.

Fig. 3.36 Turn right side out.

Fig. 3.37 Fill pillow case with stuffing and zigzag stitch it closed.

Fig. 3.38 Use Velcro across the top of the outer pillow case for a simple closure.

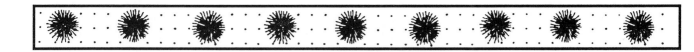

for filling—they were so comfortable! I replaced the filling in one with bean bag pellets, which made it so uncomfortable nobody wanted it, so be sure, if you make one, to use something inviting for the filling. Julie thinks we don't need any filling for her pillow—the pompoms are enough. I think she's right.

But floor pillows are terrific inventions. To make one, first sew up a pillow case lining (several inches longer and wider than the outside pillow cover), fill it with stuffing (not too tight), and sew it closed. Prepare the outer cover, using a zipper at one end or a heavy duty strip of Velcro. Then the cover can be removed and washed on occasion, or new covers can be made for the same stuffing.

When you stuff the lining into the bag you may need help, but because the lining is larger and not filled tight, the outer bag will fill up and out to the corners without a struggle.

But I've been thinking pompoms on a smaller scale, too. I've seen them sewn on sweaters along with knitted tubes (remember spool knitting?) arranged in abstract designs. A friend of mine has a pompom on a key chain so she can always find it in the bottom of her purse.

Find a knitting shop with a supply of the latest in knitting yarns. Now rethink pompoms. You'll find metallics, furs, combinations of hairy threads, and glitz—it's not just plain old 4-ply anymore.

Think large or think little. Glue pompoms on top of gripper closures in place of buttons, or on barrettes, shoe clips, or plastic headbands; think teeny and make them for earrings or sew a dozen of them around a fiber necklace. Pompoms mean fun.

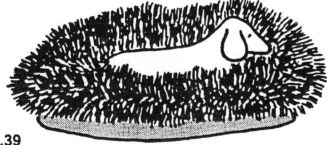

Fig. 3.39

Fig. 3.39 Otto, the family pooch, makes the pompom pillow his pet pillow.

Chapter III **Raveled, Fringed, and Looped** **73**

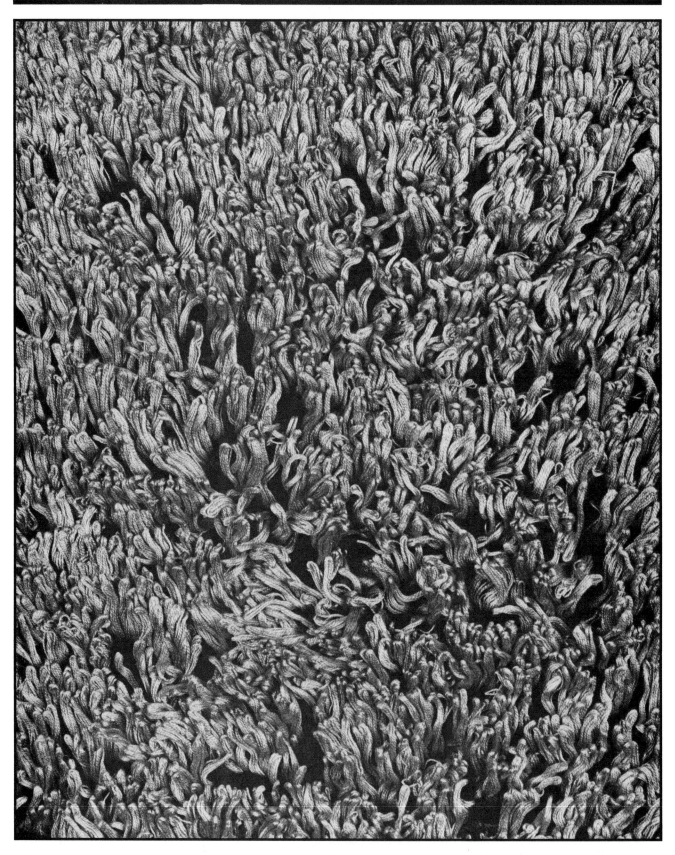

11. Upholstery Fringed Rug

Combine commercially made fringe with a backing of striped ticking for one of the simplest rugs.

Rug size: 24" X 36" (61cm X .9m)

Stitch width: 4

Stitch length: 1-1/2

Needle: #100/16 jeans

Thread: top, monofilament; bobbin, white polyester

Presser foot: no snag type (see Chapter I)

Fabric: pillow ticking for backing (stripes run short way)

Yarn: approximately 27 yards (24.5m) of 4" (10cm) red upholstery fringe, 27 yards (24.5m) black and red ball fringe (available at upholstery stores)

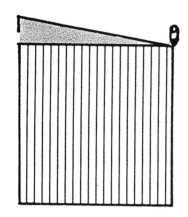

Fig. 3.40

Fig. 3.41

Fringes come in various widths and I found that if I use 4" (10cm) fringe, it's so long that the direction of the fringe at the last edge finished is not noticeable when the rug is completed. I also used a narrower black and red tassel fringe, which took the rug out of the ordinary.

The fringes are stitched to pillow ticking stripes to keep the rows of fringing straight. Another help is butting one strip of tape to the next.

Use Method 1 in Appendix A to finish the rug. Then fold the backing in half parallel to the stripes and place a safety pin at the top edge of the fold line as a marker (Fig. 3.40). Later you will turn the rug around when you reach the safety pin.

Before you begin stitching, it is helpful to cut all the fringe to the correct length, adding 1" (2.5cm) to turn under. The total length of each fringe will be 25" (63.5cm). Start with a row of black tassels. With the tassels facing left, fold under 1/2" (1.5cm) of tape, backstitch by stitching up and back at the top edge and zigzag stitch the tape to the left side edge of the rug backing (stitch width 4, stitch length 1-1/2). At the bottom, fold under the black tape again, then backstitch the tape in place (Fig. 3.41). Go back to the top, fold under a strip of red tape, butt the red tape to the edge of the black tape (red fringe also faces left), backstitch and zigzag it in place (no backing shows between tapes). Fold it under at the end and anchor it securely. If the tape is too wide and the edge lifts from the fabric even after it's stitched in place, either widen the zigzag stitches or stitch down another row of zigzags to hold the tape in place.

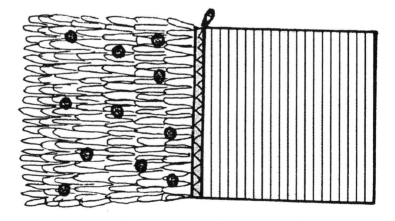

Fig. 3.42A

Continue in this manner until you reach the safety pin at the middle of the rug (Fig. 3.42A). Then change directions by

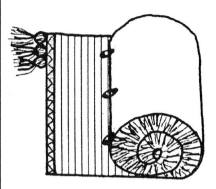

Fig. 3.43

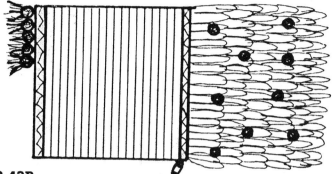

Fig. 3.42B

turning the rug around and stitching at the other side edge (Fig. 3.42B). You then work with half a bulky, fringed rug between the needle and the sewing machine. But to make it even easier, roll up the rug and pin it with safety pins (Fig. 3.43). Unroll and move the pins as you stitch the tapes in place on the other half.

Begin as before with black tape. Continue stitching the tapes down, always facing them to the left as you stitch, until you reach the center. Stitch red fringe on top of the last tape stitched down the center (Fig. 3.44).

And that's as easy as it comes when making rugs.

Hint: This sounds like an expensive rug, but it wasn't. The red upholstery fringe I used came from an upholstery outlet store where give-away prices are the norm. The black fringe and striped ticking came from a thrift store.

No matter what type of needlework you do, check out all the stores, discount houses, thrift shops, and garage sales in your area and always be on the lookout for supplies.

Fig. 3.44

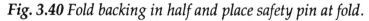

Fig. 3.40 Fold backing in half and place safety pin at fold.

Fig. 3.41 Start with tassel fringe at left edge, facing left.

Fig. 3.42
  A. After stitching down the strip at the pin, turn rug around.
  B. Turn rug around and begin stitching fringe down other side.

Fig. 3.43 Roll up and pin the completed half to make stitching easier.

Fig. 3.44 Place last fringe on top of the center strip.

Chapter III **Raveled, Fringed, and Looped** **77**

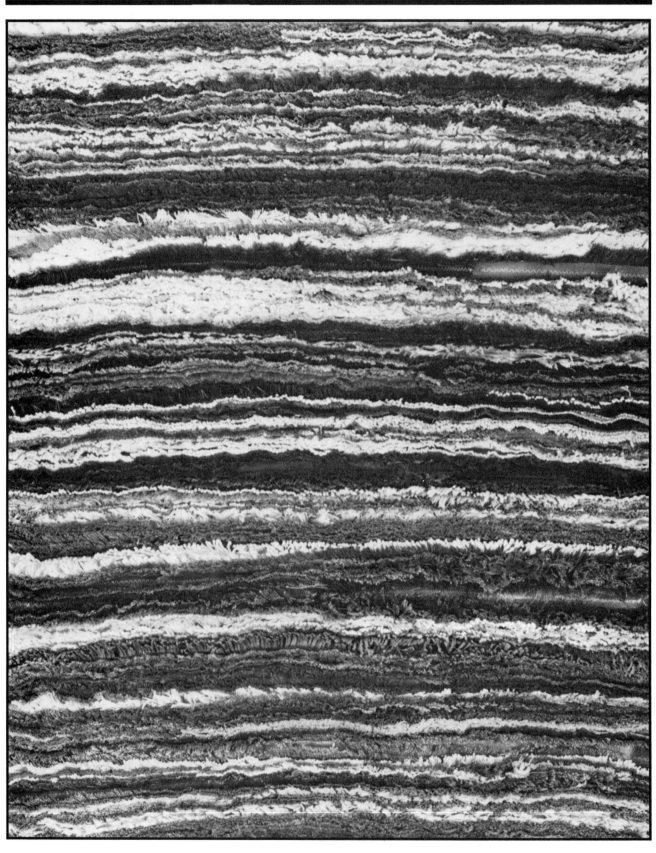

12. Fringed Linen Rug

I've been collecting linen yardage for years because I love it. It's expensive now, but you can find it at bargain prices in thrift stores—look for tablecloths and napkins.

Construction of this rug is like the denim rug in Chapter 5. The strips are stitched through the centers to attach them in close rows across the rug backing. The only difference, besides cutting these strips on the straight of grain, is that three strips are stacked together and stitched as one in this rug.

Rug size: 24" X 36" (61cm X .9m)

Stitch width: 3

Stitch length: 1-1/2

Needle: #90/14 jeans

Thread: top, monofilament; bobbin, white polyester

Presser foot: general purpose

Fabric: two 26" X 38" (66cm X 96.5cm) pieces of heavy canvas backing; linens or blends of loosely woven fabrics of different weights and colors cut in 2" (5cm) strips for fringing

Miscellaneous: rotary cutter, mat, 6" X 24" (15cm X 61cm) clear plastic ruler, permanent marker

Use a ruler, mat, and rotary cutter when cutting strips on the straight of grain, with no tearing allowed. Tearing pulls the edges so sometimes they pack together and roll, which makes fringing difficult.

The backing canvas is prepared using Method 2 in Appendix A. Using the marker and ruler, mark around all four sides 1" (2.5cm) from the edge. Go back and mark lines for stitching guides across the short side of the canvas every 1/2" (1.5cm) for stitching guides.

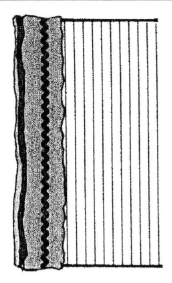

Fig. 3.45

Begin stitching at the left side of the canvas so the bulk of the rug will stay at the left of the needle as you progress. Stack three strips, then center the stack over the left edge. Always backstitch to anchor the threads at the beginning and end of each row. It's important to stitch directly down the centers (stitch width 3, stitch length 1-1/2) (Fig. 3.45). If the stitching wavers, it's not a tragedy, but when you fringe later, you may find it difficult because the thread won't pull out evenly across.

Should a strip be too short, add another next to it. Anchor again. You may wish to add a different color to finish out the line. This is fine, but don't add short strips to the ends of your lines only. Add short strips to the beginnings, too, to balance the rug color.

The colors I chose for this rug included browns and beiges, aqua and greens, which I added throughout, depending on how many strips I had of each color. Even though this rug includes only bits and pieces of scrap fabric, I took time to semi-plan the color placement. For example, I had only a few strips of aqua, and I didn't want to run out too soon, so I held back on that color. One large piece of beige linen afforded me many strips, so I included that often all across the rug.

When all the stitching is completed, fringe the strips. If the thread pulls out unevenly when fringing, cut it off before it reaches the stitching line (Fig. 3.46). In fact, the fringe should start 1/4" (6mm) from the zigzag stitched center.

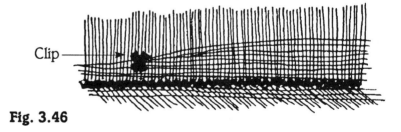

Clip

Fig. 3.46

Fig. 3.45 Stack 3 strips of fabric and stitch down to backing.

Fig. 3.46 Clip any threads 1/4" (6mm) from stitching if they pull out unevenly.

Before you sew the backing on, place the rug on a flat surface. Any fringe ends too long? The nature of the rug (stacking and stitching three layers at a time) precludes the fringes all being the same height, but you may find, because you stitched off-center, that some fringes are much too long. Clip these off to an appropriate height.

The rug top finished, use Method 2 in Appendix A to complete the rug. By placing the double backing on a rug, it makes the rug sturdier and protects the stitches.

After I completed this rug, which grew out of the Denim Chenille Mat idea (Rug #19), another idea popped into my head. It started a chain of What Ifs. To go back to the beginning—first, because the denim rug involved stitching individual strips in place and took a long time, I speeded up the process by stacking strips and stitching down several at once (Fringed Linen Rug). Then I thought, What if I don't deal in scraps? Instead, what if I use whole pieces of fabric slightly wider and longer than my intended rug? Then what if I stack five or six of those fabric pieces, stitch across at regular intervals of 2" (5cm) or so, cut them apart mid-way between stitching lines, and attach them to a backing, leaving the interval between slightly less than 2" (5cm)? I could then fringe the strips or leave them to soften up and fringe themselves in wear and washing. I've accomplished the same thing as the linen rug, but again in less time (Fig. 3.47).

Or, what if I stack the fabric, stitch at 2" (5cm) intervals, but slip a yardstick through the channel on top of the last layer of fabric and use a rotary cutter to slit through all the layers except the backing? What if?

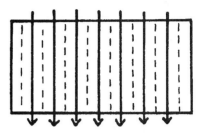

Fig. 3.47A

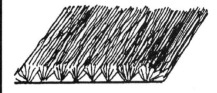

Fig. 3.47B

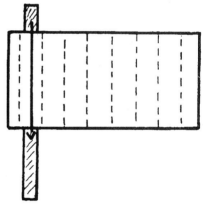

Fig. 3.48

Fig. 3.47
   A. Layer five or six whole pieces of fabric, stitch across every 2" (5cm), then cut through all the layers halfway between stitching lines.
   B. Sew strips to backing, leaving less than 2" (5cm) between strips.

Fig. 3.48 Instead of cutting completely through the strips, place a thin yardstick through the channel on top of the first layer, then cut down to the yardstick, halfway between the stitching lines.

Chapter III **Raveled, Fringed, and Looped** **81**

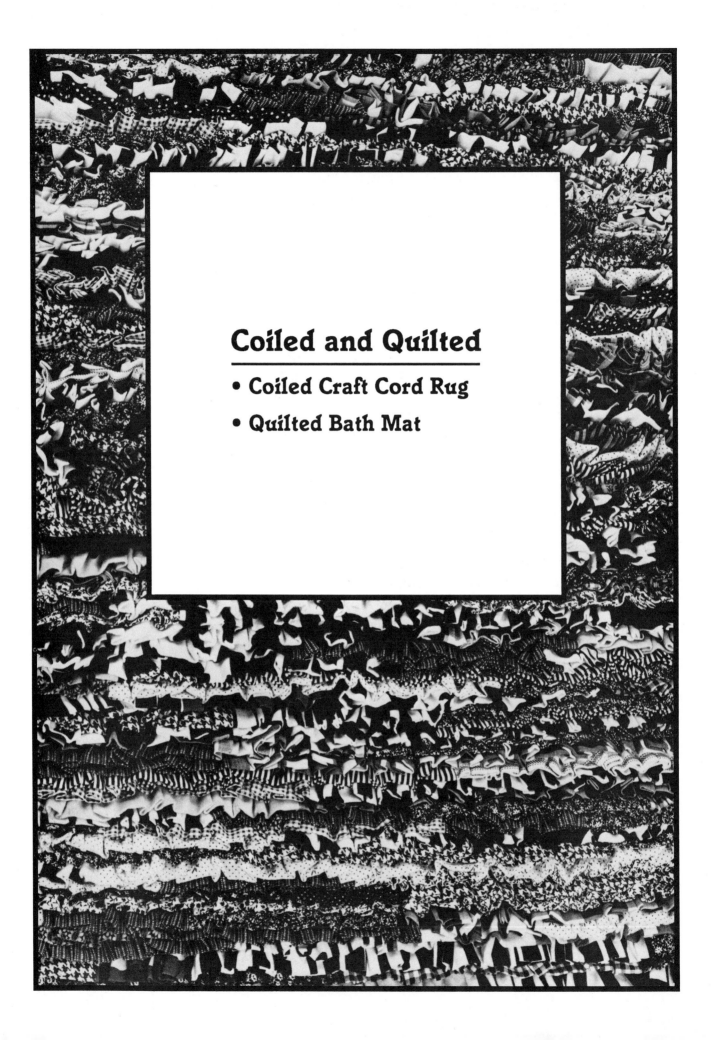

Coiled and Quilted

- Coiled Craft Cord Rug
- Quilted Bath Mat

IV. Coiled and Quilted

Place mats and crib quilts—many of us have made both. In this chapter I want you to spend a few more hours on those same techniques and make two rugs instead. These are the only two rugs in the book that aren't appliquéd, and both of them make especially appealing gifts.

The wrapped and coiled rug is made of purchased craft cord, wrapped with strips of fabric, then coiled and stitched together as you do when making a place mat.

Most directions for craft cord projects tell you to both wrap and sew at the machine, but wrapping cord and sewing it a few feet at a time is tedious and probably the reason people stop at place mats. I want you to enjoy rug making and not complain about your stiff neck or sore back the next time I see you. I insist you wrap the cord while seated in a comfortable chair—preferably while watching a favorite TV show or listening to beautiful music. When finished, take the wrapped cord to the sewing machine and finish the rug in record time. It's fun watching a place mat grow into a rug.

Filled fabric tubes can be coiled, too, as can braids. I've seen rugs made up of three bias-cut fabric strips, layered, folded the long way, then coiled and zigzag stitched together. So many rug ideas from only one method!

Sometimes quilted rugs are found next to the bed so you'll have a comfortable first step when you get up in the morning. And perhaps quilted exercise mats could be classified as rugs, too. But I thought a quilted bath mat was more practical, so I borrowed colors from our bathroom and made it decorative as well.

If you need a one-of-a-kind gift for a bride or hostess, what would be more special than this cozy bath mat to match her towels? I've always made quilts for gifts, but a rug would be more original than a quilt— and take less time. I'll never tell that it is based on a quickie reversible crib quilt I always make for baby gifts.

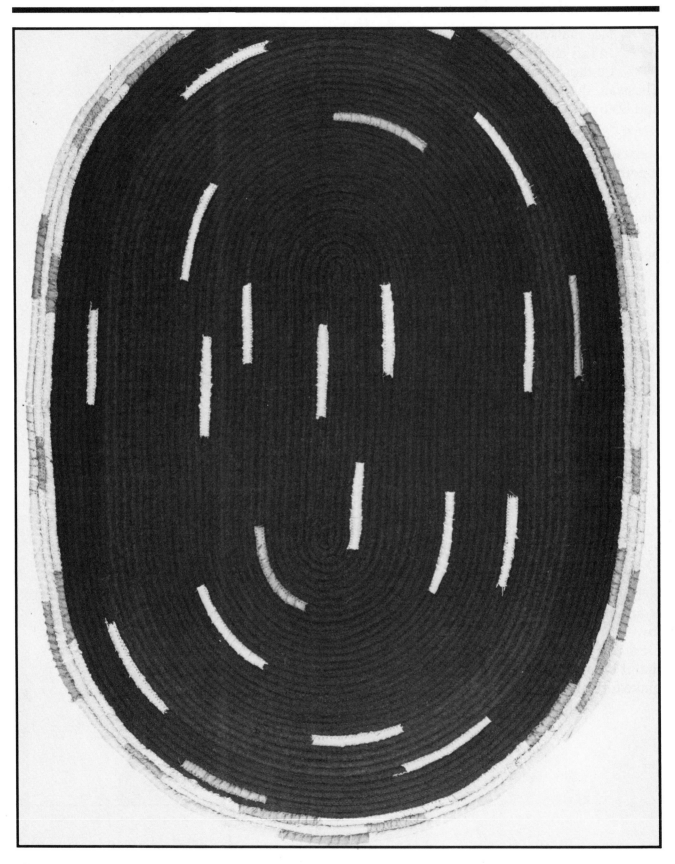

13. Coiled Craft Cord Rug

A piece of black striped fabric determined the colors in this reversible rug. I used the narrow colored stripes for the colors scattered in and bordering the rug and the large areas of black for the main color.

Beware: If you don't have a sewing-machine table to surround your machine, don't try to make this rug. It will not lie flat. The kind of small portable table where the bed folds up into place around the needle area is fine (see Sources of Supplies for Sirco tables).

Rug size: 26" X 36" (66cm X .9m)

Stitch width: 3

Stitch length: 1-1/2

Needle: #110/16 jeans

Thread: top, black polyester, monofilament; bobbin, black polyester, monofilament

Presser foot: general purpose

Fabric: striped cotton, approximately 4 yards each (3.5m) in black, red, purple, bright blue, jade

Miscellaneous: four packages (200 feet or 6m) craft cord, glue stick, dressmaker's pins, hand-sewing needle

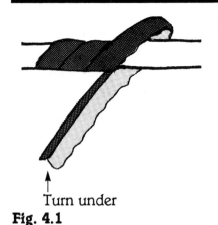

Turn under

Fig. 4.1

To create the rug, first preshrink the fabric, then clip it at 1" (2.5cm) intervals, determined by the stripes, and tear the fabric parallel to the selvage into long strips. Wrap all the cord with black strips, but leave approximately 9 yards (8m) of one hank unwrapped (for the border). To wrap the cord, fold over 1/4" (6mm) at the long edge of a black strip before you begin and while wrapping (Fig. 4.1). If you prefer, you can wrap with raw edges exposed, but I prefer folding the edge so the large black area of the rug has a clean finish. How closely you wrap is also up to you. I'm comfortable with approximately 3/8" (1cm) to 1/2" (1.5cm) wraps, though I never measure with a ruler as I wrap.

To start the first strip, pin it approximately 1" (2.5cm) from the end of the craft cord (Fig. 4.2A). Pull the strip to the end of the cord and wrap the end, enclosing the cord. Fold in the edge and wrap all the craft cord (Fig. 4.2B) (except for 9 yards) in the same manner (Fig. 4.2C).

Fig. 4.2A

Fig. 4.2B

Fig. 4.2C

Fig. 4.1 Fold under 1/4" (6mm) of fabric while wrapping the cord.

Fig. 4.2 To begin wrapping:
  A. Pin strip to cord, then pull back to end.
  B. Wrap the cord over itself to cover the end.
  C. Continue to wrap the cord.

Whenever you join one black strip to another, glue the last inch of the first strip to the craft cord. Begin the next strip by folding over the edge, dotting the underside of the end with glue, then overlapping the end of the wrapped cord, approximately 1" (2.5cm). Poke a pin through the new strip and cord at the join and keep it pinned until you complete the tight wraps.

To add craft cord, join the ends one of two ways. Cut the ends of the cords on a slant and glue to keep them from fraying (Fig. 4.3A), then join them on the slants. Pinning at the join may help, but be extremely careful not to pull them apart as you continue wrapping (Fig. 4.3B). After you cover the join with fabric, pin through the fabric and cords to hold them in place until you wrap well past the join. Or, using a hand sewing needle and thread, sew the slanted ends together by poking the needle in and out the two ends and wrapping with thread before knotting and cutting the thread (Fig. 4.3C).

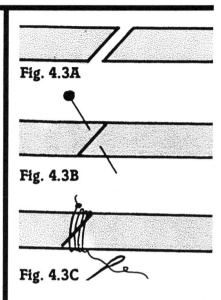

Fig. 4.3A

Fig. 4.3B

Fig. 4.3C

Fig. 4.3 To add craft cord:
A. Cut cords on slants and glue together.
B. Either use pins to help hold cords together while wrapping.
C. Or hand stitch through the cords and wrap with thread to hold in place.

Start here —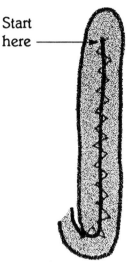

Fig. 4.4

Once the cord is wrapped with black fabric, it's time to sew the rug together. This must be done on a flat surface. Don't use the free arm of your sewing machine or even the small flat-bed extensions that are attached to the machine. I tried to do this, and no matter what I did to stitch it flat, I still had a domed rug (which could be exaggerated, to make a basket). By placing my machine in a sewing table I had no trouble keeping the rug flat.

Always work with the bulk of your rug to the left of the machine. Begin the first row of stitching (black thread on top and bobbin) in the middle of the rug (Fig. 4.4). Turn 12" (30.5cm) length of wrapped cord back on itself. Don't leave the needle in the fabric. Raise the presser bar lever. Then turn the cord to the right and push it snuggly next to the first row of cord. Continue stitching clockwise, the rug always to the left of the needle (Fig. 4.5). As you stitch, keep your eye on the midline of the presser foot and keep that directly over the space between the cords so the zigzag stitch catches both cords. Widen the zigzag if you wish, but don't narrow the stitch width to less than 3mm.

Color is added to the rug over the black as it's stitched together, so you have control over where the color occurs. (See color pages.) Prepare the strips by cutting them into 12" (30.5cm) lengths. The colored areas, wrapped over the black, are bulkier, so keep the wraps farther apart and don't fold under the long edge.

Fig. 4.4 Start stitching from curve to start of craft cord.

Dot the end of the colored strip with glue stick and place it on the black cord. Fold over the end once to finish it, then wrap to the end of the strip and glue to the black cord.

The border starts where the craft cord is unwrapped. To add three colored rows for the border, change to monofilament thread on top and bobbin to prevent black stitches from showing. Although the colors are used in order (jade, bright blue, red, purple), cut the strips at different lengths as you wrap and try to stitch so the colors on adjoining cords don't match (sometimes they overlap). To control those colors, wrap and stitch the last three rows while sitting at the machine, stitching as you wrap. When finished, cut the cord on an opposite slant, then glue and hand-stitch the strip to hold it in place. Stitch it again by machine to finish the rug.

I didn't use every inch of the cord in the four hanks. I wrapped until I reached the size rug I wanted, then added the border. I hope from this estimate, you will be able to estimate the size of your own rug.

Now hold the rug up to a light. Did your stitching miss places? This happens, but it's no problem to go back and stitch the cords together later—it won't show.

Stitch clockwise

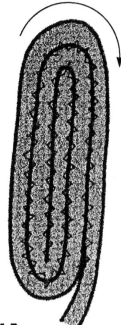

Fig. 4.5

Fig. 4.5 Continue stitching in a clockwise direction.

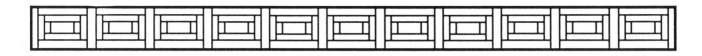

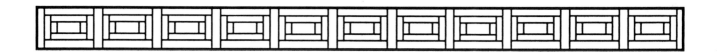

14. Quilted Bath Mat

It took me only one day to construct this rug on my sewing machine. If you have a serger, you can break my speed record.

Rug size: 32" X 37" (81.5cm X 94cm)

Stitch width: 0 – 3

Stitch length: 1-1/2 – 2

Needle: #110/16 jeans

Thread: top, monofilament; bobbin, monofilament

Presser foot: no snag type or general purpose foot

Fabric: towels:
> One patterned hand towel
> (piece: 11" X 16" (28cm X 40.5cm))
>
> One beige bath towel
> (four strips: 3-1/2" X 10-1/2" (9cm X 26cm))
> (two strips: 8" X 27" (20.5cm X 68.5cm))
>
> One rose bath towel
> (four strips: 3-1/2" X 22" (9cm X 56cm))
> (two strips: 8" X 36" (20.5cm X .9m))
>
> One blue bath towel
> (One piece: 11" X 16" (28cm X 40.5cm))
> (Two strips: 4-3/4" X 41" (12cm X 1m))
> (Two strips: 4-3/4" X 37" (12cm X .9m))
>
> One patterned bath towel
> (two strips: 8" X 27" (20.5cm X 68.5cm))
> (two strips: 8" X 36" (20.5cm X .9m)

Miscellaneous: large-sized rotary cutter and mat, 6" X 24" (15cm X 61cm) clear plastic ruler, strips of bonded batting the same sizes as the strips, hand-sewing needle

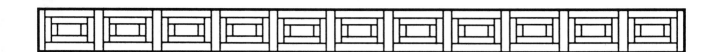

This bath mat is reversible and constructed so both sides are completed at the same time. What better way to coordinate a color scheme than to use towels that match those in the bathroom? One word of warning: don't choose heavy velour. As you sew the rug, you'll soon understand. Indeed, the rug gets so thick at places that velour wouldn't fit under the presser foot. (For other helpful hints, see end of directions.)

It is most interesting to start with a patterned towel because you can choose colors for the other strips by matching those in the pattern. You may have a difficult time matching colors, so do all of your buying at one time.

The bath mat is constructed log-cabin style (Courthouse Steps) (Fig. 4.6), and with any log-cabin pattern, there is always a center patch. Before I bought the towels, I found a hand towel with an interesting design I could use as a center motif, as well as decorative bands on the matching bath towels that I could use as the last strips around the rug.

The patterned bath towels I chose had bands of the design 8" (22.5cm) wide down each side. When I cut out the bands, I was mindful that I also needed 1/4" (6mm) on each side for seaming.

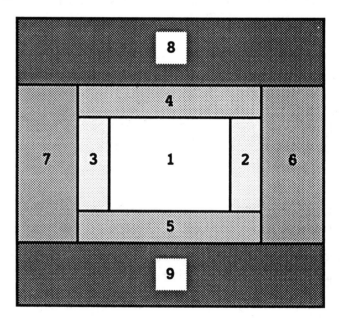

Fig. 4.6

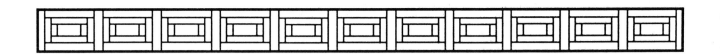

While planning the topside, remember that you must plan the back of the towel as well—this is a reversible rug. Check Fig. 4.6 to see my arrangement. Use plain colors or only one color for the reverse. I used blue, in the center, beige on the short sides, rose on the long sides.

To begin cutting strips, cut off any towel hems and throw them away. You may use the selvages for seam allowances so leave those in place. Next, when you cut out strips, measure only the width needed plus seam allowances, leaving the rest the lengths of the towels.

The length of each strip is shown at the beginning of the directions, but only the side measurements are important to you when you construct the rug. For that reason, with the exception of the centerpieces, only the width measurement of the strips is mentioned from now on. This is because the full-length strips are added to the rug, stitched, then cut off as you proceed.

The hand towel was cut down to include only the center, patterned area and the 1/4" (6mm) seam allowance. The result was a piece of towel measuring 11" X 16" (28cm X 40.5cm). Then cut out the same size piece from a solid blue hand towel for the underside. Sandwich a piece of bonded batting (without any seam allowance, to cut down on bulk) between the two towel pieces (wrong sides together) (Fig. 4.7A). (The batting won't slip and is held in place by quilting stitches later.) Straight stitch 1/4" (6mm) from the edges around the sandwich. Then go back and zigzag the edges together to keep them flat (Fig. 4.7B).

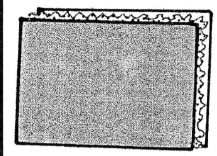

Fig. 4.7A

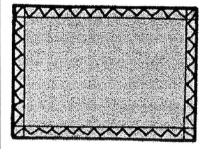

Fig. 4.7B

Fig. 4.6 Stitch quilted rug in this order.

Fig. 4.7
 A. Sandwich batting between top and backing.
 B. Straight stitch, then zigzag around all four sides.

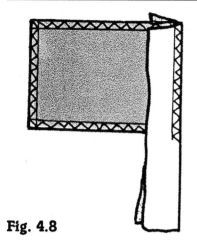

Fig. 4.8

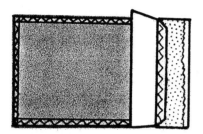

Fig. 4.9

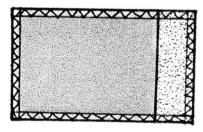

Fig. 4.10

Next, sandwich the center piece between two beige short-side strips (3-1/2" (9cm) wide), arranging the short strips at the edge with top sides facing the center (Fig. 4.8). The strips will be longer than the center piece. Straight stitch the seam; then go back and zigzag over the edge. Do the same at the other side. Cut the strips even with the edge of the center piece. At each side seam, trim off the corners. Smooth out one of the bottom strips, then slip in a piece of batting (this should extend into the seam allowances at the short sides) (Fig. 4.9) and smooth the top piece over it. Stitch the three sides closed (Fig. 4.10).

To eliminate bulk in the seams of all the strips, place the batting between long seam allowances, catching it in only the short side seam allowances.

Next, sides 4 and 5 (3-1/2" or 9cm wide) are stitched in place. Both top and undersides are rose. Then sides 6 and 7 (8" or 20.5cm wide) are added as you did the others. The topsides are patterned, the undersides, beige. The last sides to stitch are 8 and 9 (8" or 20.5cm wide). The topsides on the last strips are patterned, the undersides rose.

Fig. 4.8 Add side 2 as shown.

Fig. 4.9 Slip in batting, catching it only at top and bottom.

Fig. 4.10 Straight stitch, then zigzag all 3 sides.

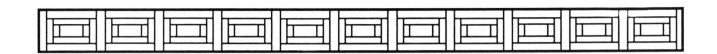

Once the rug is finished this far, take a look at it. Unlike a true log cabin, the strips in this rug are different widths, determined by the design on the towels. The patterned areas are too large to leave unquilted if I follow the quilting rule of thumb: no unquilted space should be larger than your hand. It's especially true for a rug, as you want to produce a stiffer, rather than softer feel. If your strips are too wide, then quilt inside them.

As an example, I outline stitched the center motif (Fig. 4.11). This transfers the design to the plain center piece on the reverse side and holds the batting in place as well.

The narrow 3" (7.5cm) strips (strips 2 through 5) remain unquilted.

But my patterned pieces are 8" (20.5cm) wide, which is much too large to be attractive unquilted. The color change in the design makes the strip look as though it were divided in half the long way, so I chose that invisible dividing line for my quilting stitches.

Consider these other ideas for quilting the rug: stitch approximately 1/4" (6mm) in from the seam line around each strip (Fig. 4.12A); bisect a strip the long way (Fig. 4.12B); or stitch perpendicular lines across the strips, creating squares along the length (Fig. 4.12C).

Fig. 4.11

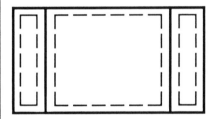

Fig. 4.12A

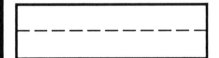

Fig. 4.12B

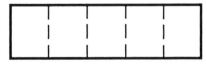

Fig. 4.12C

Fig. 4.11 Stitch around design motifs.

Fig. 4.12
  A. Quilt 1/4" (6mm) inside from each seam.
  B. Bisect strip with quilting.
  C. Quilt to divide large open spaces.

Chapter IV **Coiled and Quilted** **95**

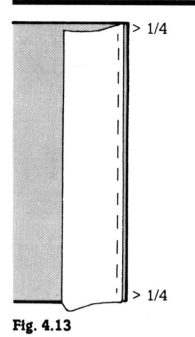

Fig. 4.13

Finally, place the blue binding on top, front side of the binding strip to the top side edge of the rug. Straight stitch 1/4" (6mm) from the edge starting 1/4" (6mm) from the top and ending 1/4" (6mm) from the bottom (Fig. 4.13). Fold binding around to back, leaving 1-1/2" (4cm) of binding showing on top (Fig. 4.14). Turn under the raw edge to meet the fold underneath. Pin in place (Fig. 4.15). Fold in the top and bottom edges (leave 1/4" (6mm) exposed at top and bottom of the mat) (Fig. 4.16). Stitch the binding by hand along the edges and at each end. Completely finish the bindings on both sides, then repeat these directions for the top and bottom edges (but stitch those bindings on all across the top and bottom). After you finish stitching the bindings, join them to the side bindings with hand stitches (Fig. 4.17).

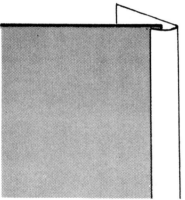

Fig. 4.14

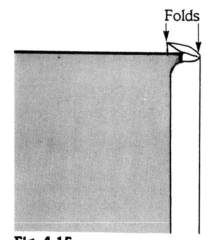

Fig. 4.15

Fig. 4.13 Stitch bindings to rug sides beginning and ending 1/4" (6mm) from top and bottom.

Fig. 4.14 Wrap binding around edge.

Fig. 4.15 Fold in edge of binding 1-1/2" (4cm) to meet fold.

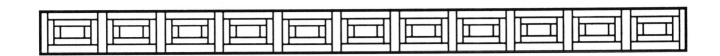

H int: This rug is super simple to make, but use these helpful reminders: Don't use velour. Trim all corners. Don't stitch batting into the long side seam allowances. Let the machine feed the fabric all by itself to prevent broken needles. When you come to a place that is too bulky to stitch, lift the presser foot and move it over the bulk as you hand feed the needle.

Towels are expensive. Fortunately, I found these at a linen outlet store, so the mat cost about half what I expected to pay. Terry cloth fabric is less expensive than buying towels, so to save even more money, buy your fabric by the yard, not the towel.

Fig. 4.16

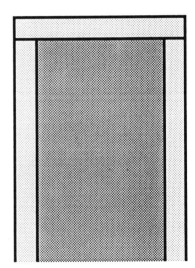

Fig. 4.17

Fig. 4.16 At top and bottom, poke the bindings to the inside.

Fig. 4.17 Stitch binding across top and bottom and stitch to side bindings to finish.

Chapter IV **Coiled and Quilted** **97**

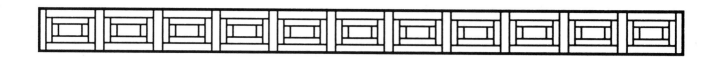

Here is Cate Keller's idea to make an even faster quilted bath mat: find a sensational bath towel that lends itself to quilting, but don't cut or piece anything. Find a plain towel for the backing. If it has a tightly woven decorative strip near the bottom edge, cut it off because once the towel is washed, it has a tendency to pull in at that place. Cut a piece of light batting the same size as the towels.

Stripes and plaids are simple—you can quilt the straight lines in a flash—but towels like the one I used in this chapter work well, too. The quilting lines are straight.

If you're daring or already know how simple free-machine quilting is and want to quilt a flowered towel, for example, then use the darning foot (darning springs or open free-embroidery feet get tangled in the terry loops), lower or cover the feed dogs, loosen tension slightly (remember that all machines are different and this may vary from one machine to the next), and use monofilament thread on top and bobbin unless you can find a good towel match in polyester sewing thread.

To quilt using the general purpose or zigzag foot, remember to use a matching thread or monofilament, keep feed dogs up, use normal tension, and stitch at a normal stitch length (2-1/2) or slightly longer.

Before you begin quilting freely or with the presser foot on, decide how you will finish the edges:

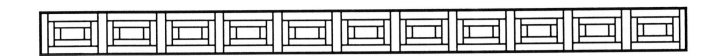

Method 1: Cut off the hems on both towels. Make a sandwich of the plain towel on bottom, the batting in the middle, and the decorative towel on top. Use large safety pins to pin-baste the layers together—no farther than a hand apart. Press down and out at both sides of the presser foot to keep the fabric taut as you quilt freely. This is not as important if you quilt with the feed dogs up and the general purpose presser foot on. Finish the rug with bindings as shown previously in the chapter.

Method 2: This method eliminates the bindings. First, cut off the towel hems. You may want to baste the batting to the back of the plain towel at this time.

Now place the plain towel on a table with batting next to the table. Place the decorative towel on top, topside inside. Pin together. Then stitch around three sides like a pillow case. If you have a serger this is a good time to use it. On the fourth side, stitch past the corners on both sides for a few inches.

Clip corners back and trim the seam allowances at those points to eliminate bulk. Turn this bag to the right side, encasing the batting. Whip stitch or ladder stitch (see Snowflake Rug) to close.

Flatten the quilt and pin baste it together with large safety pins. Quilt the layers together freely or with feed dogs in place.

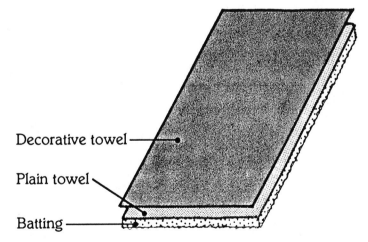

Decorative towel

Plain towel

Batting

Fig. 4.18

Fig. 4.18 Stack the towels: batting underneath, plain towel (topside up) in the middle, decorative towel on top (topside down).

Chapter IV **Coiled and Quilted** **99**

Scraps and Strips

- Amish Doubleknit
  Dust Catcher

- Squares and Triangles Rug

- Caterpillar Rug

- Shirred Carmen Miranda Rug

- Denim Chenille Mat

- Flat Folds and Clipped
  Strips Chair Rug

V. Scraps and Strips

What a blessing! I've discovered rugs made from scraps and strips. It's the answer to my fabric-buying habit and I've actually made a dent in my fabric stash. In fact, I never knew my fabric "mistakes" could look so good.

Before you decide on a rug to make, prepare samples of each. Even then you may not know which rug to make first because they each have a personality you can't resist.

Included in this chapter are the Amish Doubleknit Dust Catcher and the Squares and Triangles Rug. Each are made from small fabric scraps; the difference in their look comes from the way the scraps are manipulated and attached to the backing.

Strip rugs have long histories (see Appendix C). Like the patch scraps, the method used to prepare and stitch down the strips determines the look and name of the rug.

If you're a fabric lover, this will be your favorite chapter.

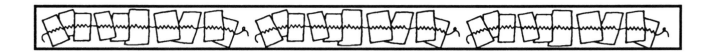

15. Amish Double-knit Dust Catcher

This is a traditional Amish item, which is why I retained the name. But if you frequent fiber galleries as I do, you know that a favorite title for fiber pieces is "Homage to (Something)," or "(Something) Revisited." The first thing that popped into my head when I saw these remnants spilled onto a table was "Homage to the Revisited 1960s." The fabric is '60s; even the colors are '60s. If you threw out all your polyester doubleknit with your bell bottoms, then do as I did: I actually bought more doubleknit! In fact, for 65 cents I bought 25 yards (23m) of doubleknit at a church rummage sale. My problem is—I have enough to make at least 10 more rugs.

It's called a dust catcher, because you can just pick them up and shake out the dust. Best of all, once you cut your colors, you can stitch this rug in an afternoon.

Rug Size: 20" X 32" (51cm X 81.5cm)

Stitch width: 0 – 3

Stitch length: 1-1/2

Needle: #100/16 jeans

Thread: top, monofilament; bobbin, orange polyester

Presser foot: general purpose

Fabric: orange polyester doubleknit for backing—two pieces, each 20" X 32" (51cm X 81.5cm); scraps 1/2 yard (46cm) each: yellow, pink, fuchsia, turquoise, white, apple green

Miscellaneous: rotary cutter and mat, 6" X 24" (15cm X 61cm) clear plastic ruler, marker, fusible webbing 20" X 32" (51cm X 81.5cm)

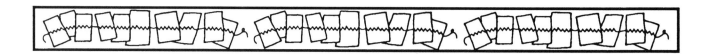

First prepare the backing by cutting two pieces of doubleknit, each 20" X 32" (51cm X 81.5cm). Use a fusible webbing such as Stitch Witchery or Wonder-Under to fuse the two pieces together to make it sturdier. It's not necessary to mark every stitching line so I prefer to mark a guide line every 2" (5cm) across the backing.

Cut up other polyester remnants into 2" X 4" (5cm X 10cm) rectangles. Beginning at the left side of the backing (I prefer working from left to right to keep the rug's bulk at my left), place the center of the first rectangle at the edge of the backing, anchor the threads, then zigzag down through the center (stitch width 3, stitch length 1-z1/2), dividing the scrap into 2" X 2" (5cm X 5cm) flaps (Fig. 5.1). Place another scrap of another color at the left edge, next to or slightly overlapping the first and stitch this in place as you did the first. Continue with the other colors until you reach the bottom of the edge, without placing two scraps of the same color together. Backstitch at the end, anchoring the threads.

Go back to the top and fold back the first row of scraps to the left (Fig. 5.2). Begin stitching another row about 1/4" (6mm) from the first row of stitches. To measure easily, use the presser foot as a guide: keep the side of the foot butted up to the stitches on the previous row. Even though the stitching continues in straight lines, vary the angle of the scraps and slip some scraps under instead of over the scrap you're stitching, if you wish. Then the rug doesn't look too consistent and boring. Continue until you've covered the backing entirely. The last row ends on the edge.

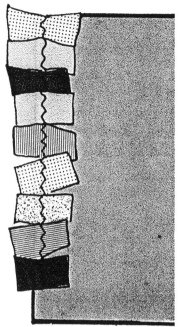

Fig. 5.1

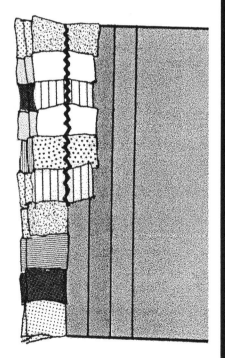

Fig. 5.2

Fig. 5.1 Stitch down center of rectangles to apply to backing.

Fig. 5.2 Flip right half to left, then stitch down the next row of rectangles.

104 Machine-Made Rugs Chapter V

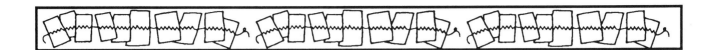

I've seen this rug made in cotton, leather and suede. Tightly woven woolen would be an excellent choice. Pink edges or cut the scraps in larger or smaller sizes (Fig. 5.3A). Try circles instead of rectangles (Fig. 5.3B), or fold the rectangles in half first, then stitch down on the fold (Fig. 5.3C).

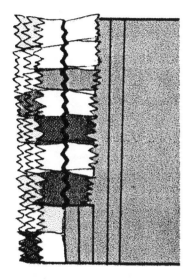

Fig. 5.3A

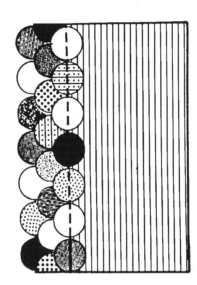

Fig. 5.3B

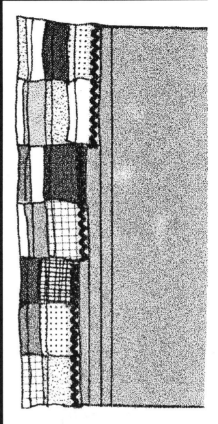

Fig. 5.3C

Fig. 5.3
A. Pink ends of rectangles before applying them.
B. Attach circles instead of rectangles.
C. Fold rectangles first, then stitch in place.

16. Squares and Triangles Rug

The history of this rug goes back to the early twentieth century when penny and pen wiper rugs were first made. The different looks of these scrap patch rugs depend on how the patches are stitched down to the backing. When a 6-year-old friend of mine saw this rug in progress, her comment was, "Butterflies!" Indeed, if you attach scraps using the following method, the points of the triangles stand up like wings.

Rug Size: 22" X 34" (56cm X 86cm)

Stitch width: 0

Stitch length: 2

Needle: #90/14 jeans

Thread: top, monofilament; bobbin, white polyester

Presser foot: general purpose

Fabric: 24" X 36" (61cm X .9m) pillow ticking for backing (stripes run the long way), knit fabrics—2-1/2 yards (2m) total of various colors of 60" (1.5m) wide fabric (mauve, purple, blue, fuchsia, white—use any knit blend that doesn't curl)

Miscellaneous: rotary cutter and mat, 6" X 24" (15cm X 61cm) ruler, large glue stick

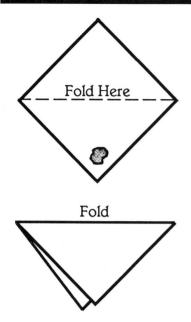

Fold Here

Fold

Fig. 5.4

Fig. 5.5

Choose fabrics that won't wrinkle when cleaned or washed. Knits were my choice because they don't wilt, don't fray easily, and can be manipulated easily during the rug construction, then thrown into a washing machine and dryer for cleaning.

Use Method 1 in Appendix A to prepare the rug backing.

It's difficult to estimate the yardage for a rug like this, but I ran a sample first and found I needed 12 squares for every 2" (5cm) square area of rug backing. In other words, I need a piece of knit fabric 2" X 24" (5cm X 61cm) for each 2" (5cm) square area on my rug. I bought 1/2 yard (46cm) each of five colors, steering clear of knits that roll, as they're too hard to work with.

To begin, place fabric on the mat, measure, and cut out long 2" (5cm) strips. Go back and cut these strips into 2" (5cm) squares. Place all of the squares into a plastic bag or box.

Take your bag of squares and a glue stick to a comfortable chair so you can relax while completing the next steps. Put dots of glue at the inside points of knit squares, fold squares into triangles (Fig. 5.4), then put the folded triangles into another bag.

Next, glue the triangles into strips (Fig. 5.5). As you glue, avoid attaching two of the same colors together. Place each triangle under and half-way down from the one before it. Don't make the strips longer than 12" (30.5cm) because it will be difficult to sew them in a straight line later.

Fig. 5.4 Dot with glue. Then fold squares in half to make triangles.

Fig. 5.5 Glue triangles into strips.

When the strips are completed, stack them next to the machine, points on top. With points on the topside, you have an invisible guideline to follow as you stitch each strip in place. Also, by tucking folds underneath, there are no folds to run into with the presser foot as you sew them down.

Place the top, folded edge of the first strip at the left top edge of the backing (on the first ticking stripe), backstitch to lock the threads, then straight stitch down through the center of the triangles until you reach the last triangle in the strip (Fig. 5.6). Stitch halfway down the triangle, then slip another strip underneath. Arrange it so the points fall on top of the stripe and continue stitching and adding strips until you get to the last triangle at the bottom edge of the rug. Fold the point under itself, with the fold on the edge of the rug, and stitch down, backstitching at the end to anchor the threads (Fig. 5.7).

To coax the triangles to stand up, position each row 3/4" (2cm) away from the previous one. Measure the distance from the first row, and note how many stripes between rows. Then instead of measuring each row, merely count stripes for placement. Before you add more strips, it helps to mark all the stitching lines with a dot of colored ink.

As you stitch each succeeding row after the first, push aside the wings of the row before it so they aren't caught in the stitches (Fig. 5.8).

Once you have sewn all the triangles to the rug, it's ready to take flight.

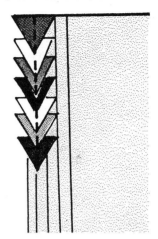

Fig. 5.6

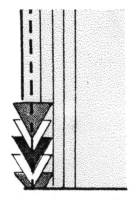

Fig. 5.7

Fig. 5.8

Fig. 5.6 Stitch straight lines of strips to the backing.

Fig. 5.7 Fold under the point of the last triangle.

Fig. 5.8 Push the first row of triangles to the left and stitch down the next row 3/4" (2cm) from the first.

Chapter V **Scraps and Strips** **109**

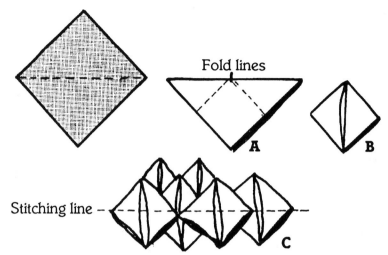

More circles, squares, and triangles: Tongues, pen wipers, shoe heels—it's not just the names that are interesting. I'm interested in the textures I can create from not only different shapes, but folding the same shapes in different ways. And it doesn't end there: I can vary the way I sew down the same shape (folded the same way) and I'll get different looks.

Sometimes these scraps are made from silk and applied to clothing. Other times they are made from felt and used under tables (where they are protected from traffic), on top of tables, or as wall hangings.

I'm making a Penny, Spool, and Dollar rug for the wall of a child's room. The name of the rug came from the three circle sizes used. My felt wall hanging combines dazzling colors— fuchsia, orange, pink, purple, and red. I preferred a heavy felt (there are many different grades), but the colors were limited, so I backed the larger circles with iron-on interfacing to make them stiffer.

To prepare the backing, I drew a grid on a piece of fuchsia felt (I used chalk I can brush off later). At intersecting lines I'll sew plain, but bright-colored

Fig. 5.9
A. Fold a square into a triangle.
B. Fold side corners down to bottom point.
C. arrange points and stitch through centers as shown.

Fig. 5.10 Grasp the fabric square in the center and gather at the point. Arrange and stitch across at the tops of the points as shown.

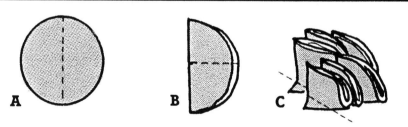

Fig. 5.11
A. Fold circle in half on dotted lines.
B. Fold again.
C. Overlap and stitch scraps to backing.

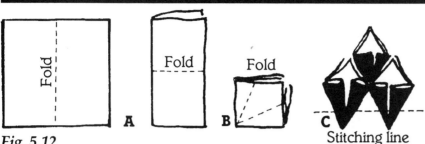

Fig. 5.12

A. *Fold a square into a rectangle, then into another square.*
B. *Then fold corners in as shown.*
C. *Stitch across folds near points.*

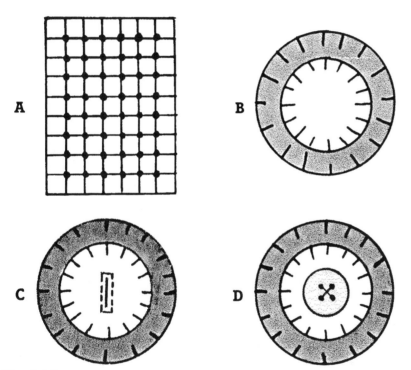

Fig. 5.13

A. *With chalk or vanishing marker, draw a graph on the felt backing; sew a button at each intersection to hold the circles in place.*
B. *Layer the felt circles, attaching the smaller spool circles to the larger dollar circles with hand-made buttonhole stitches. Work stitches around the larger circle for decoration.*
C. *With the sewing machine, straight stitch small rectangles in the centers of the circles for buttonholes. Cut through center of the rectangle.*
D. *Button to the wall hanging. The child who receives this can change the design by unbuttoning the circles and rearranging them.*

clothing buttons (sour lemon, chartreuse, turquoise).

Then, using all the felt colors, I'll cut out circles the size of a silver dollar and others the size of a large wooden spool (years ago there were stamps to do this so every circle was perfect). I'll have to cut them out by hand. No matter, all my less than perfect cuts will be covered by stitches. First I'll make stacks of one large and one small circle, doing my best to vary the color combinations, though there will be duplicates. (At least I won't place circles of the same colors together). Then I'll attach the smaller circles to the centers of the larger ones by dotting the centers lightly with glue to hold while I buttonhole stitch around the edge with pearl cotton or yarn (this can match or contrast with the circle colors). The outer edge of the larger circle is buttonhole stitched, also, for decoration.

To attach the circles to the backing, I'll need buttonholes in the centers of each circle. To do this I'll straight stitch a rectangle large enough for the buttons, then cut through the centers of each buttonhole and button the circles on to the backing.

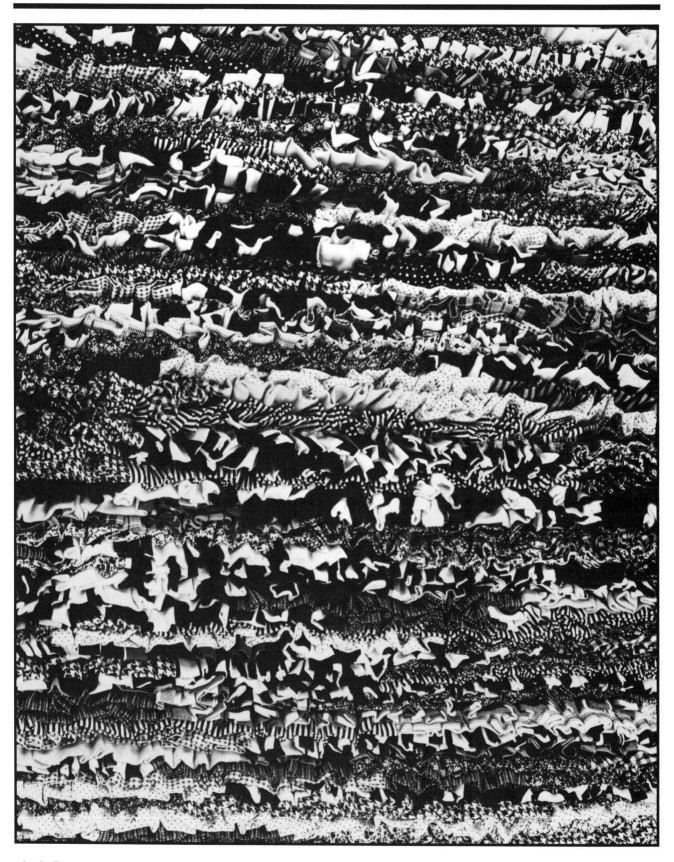

17. Caterpillar Rug

Caterpillar—what a descriptive word for a rug made from gathered tubes of fabric. Depending on how closely they are stitched to each other on the backing determines whether they stand up straight or look like overlapped ruffles.

Rug size: 24" X 36" (61cm X .9m)

Stitch width: 3

Stitch length: 1-1/2

Needle: #90/14 jeans

Thread: gimp, cordonnet, or #5 pearl cotton in fabric colors; top and bobbin, monofilament or polyester in fabric colors

Presser foot: cording or open embroidery

Fabric: cotton/poly blends 2-1/2" (6.5cm) wide strips cut on straight of grain (I used approximately 11 yards (10m) of scraps), 26" X 40" (66cm X 1m) canvas backing

Miscellaneous: rotary cutter and mat; 6" X 24" (15cm X 61cm) clear, plastic ruler; glue stick

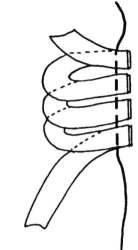

Fig. 5.14

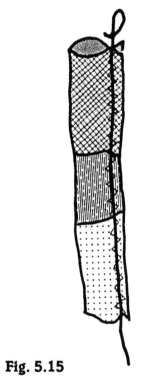

Fig. 5.15

Prepare backing as in Method 1 in Appendix A. Then cut the canvas in two: cut one side 26" X 18" (66cm X 46cm); the other is then 26" X 20" (66cm X 51cm). Mark each with guidelines every 2" (5cm) across the short side.

Cut fabric strips and then sew them together into one long strip by overlapping short ends and stitching. I do this easily and quickly by stitching from one join to the next without anchoring or leaving thread between the strips (Fig. 5.14). After completing this step, snip the thread between joins and open out the strip. Then cut the strip into 72" (1.8m) lengths. (I used 100 strips.)

To gather the strips, thread the gimp or pearl cotton through the cording foot from the front and tie a knot at the end to keep it from slipping back out. Leave a long tail. Keep the ball of gimp in your lap. Fold each strip in half the long way, wrong sides together, and place the raw edges directly under the right edge of the cording foot. Zigzag over the cord. Run one strip after the other without cutting between (Fig. 5.15). Don't overlap the fabric, though. Continue until you have added gathering cords to all the strips.

Once all the tubes are prepared, take them to an easy chair and relax while you pull up the gathers and make 24" (61cm) caterpillars. To gather the strips, pull up on the gimp between strips 1 and 2. This will make a loop. Cut the gimp in the middle and knot the cord at the top of strip 2. Go back to strip 1 and pull up on the cord until the caterpillar is about 24" (61cm) (no need to be exact). Tie a knot. Then go back to strip 2 and 3. Pull up on the gimp between, cut, tie a knot at the top of strip 3, go back to 2, and pull up to gather. Then knot. Continue in this manner until all the caterpillars are gathered.

Fig. 5.14 Sew strips together, one after another, topside to topside.

Fig. 5.15 Sew 72" (1.8m) long strips into tubes by zigzagging over cord at the long, cut edges.

Place the first caterpillar at the left-hand edge of one piece of backing. Let the fold extend about halfway beyond the edge and arrange the gathers evenly from top to bottom. Zigzag over the raw edges of the caterpillar to attach it to the backing. Add strips one after another, each about 1/4" (6mm) from the previous caterpillar (Fig. 5.16). The 2" (5cm) marks on the backing will help you keep your lines straight. Add strips up to and as close to the cut edge as possible. Cut off any backing extending beyond the stitching on the last ruffle.

When you finish the first side, go back and do the other half of the rug. First mark a line 2" (5cm) from the cut edge (the other edges are folded under). Start at the opposite folded edge. Apply caterpillars up to the 2" (5cm) mark. Slip this side under and as close as you can to the last caterpillar on the other side and pin in place (Fig. 5.17). From the top-side, straight stitch between as many rows as you can to attach one side of the backing to the other.

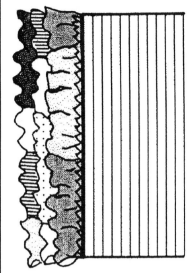

Fig. 5.16

Fig. 5.17

If you wish, protect your stitching by preparing another piece of canvas as in Method 1 in Appendix A and then attaching it to the back of the rug, hand stitching the edges together.

Idea: If you have a ruffler/pleater attachment for your machine, you may want to fold the fabric the long way, then run the strips through the accessory, pleating or ruffling the raw edges. (You won't need to use the gimp to gather the fabric.) See the Carmen Miranda Rug for another gathering idea.

Fig. 5.16 Starting at the left-hand side, apply each gathered strip to the backing.

Fig. 5.17 Attach two halves together by overlapping one with the other.

Chapter V **Scraps and Strips** 115

18. Shirred Carmen Miranda Rug

I have notebooks full of food recipes, and on the cards I write names of the friends who gave me the recipes: Mary's Cheesecake, Bev's Marinated Carrots, etc. I thought of this when I looked at the shirred rug and named it: Carmen Miranda's Rug. Not only are the colors "Carmen," but the technique of gathering strips through the centers and attaching them to a backing is one I used on Carmen Miranda sleeves for a grade school talent show. Yet this rug is rooted in American history. Shirred strips (this is like an upside-down caterpillar) have been used for rugs for over 100 years. Although usually made with tightly woven wools, I used cotton blends that stay perky and don't scrunch up when washed.

Rug size: 23" X 36" (58.5cm X .9cm)

Stitch width: 3

Stitch length: 1 – 4

Needle: #90/14 jeans

Thread: top, monofilament; bobbin, white polyester; gimp, cordonnet or #5 pearl cotton in fabric colors

Presser foot: cording or open embroidery foot

Fabric: approx. 100 yards (91.5m) of 2" (5cm) wide bias strips of cotton; 25" X 38" (63.5cm X 96.5cm) striped pillow ticking

Miscellaneous: rotary cutter and board, 6" X 24" (15cm X 61cm) clear plastic ruler, appliqué or rug (machine embroidery) scissors, Magic Tape (optional)

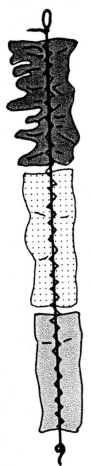

Fig. 5.18

When you make this rug you can rid yourself of fabric mistakes you've purchased, the colors from another era, or prints no longer fashionable, as only the top edges and a tiny bit of the fabric are visible. Your eyes see a blend, so prints, plaids and stripes become colors, not designs.

I forget why I purchased the wild, striped fabric I never used, so I decided to get rid of it in this rug. The stripe colors dictated the other colors I chose.

To construct the rug, use the ruler, rotary cutter and mat to cut 2"-wide (5cm) strips on the bias.

Prepare the backing by using Method 1 in Appendix A, using pillow ticking—stripes running across the backing the short way.

To make ruffles, thread a cord such as gimp, cordonnet or pearl cotton through the cording foot from the front and tie a knot at the end of the cord. If you don't have a cording foot, use any presser foot that has space underneath (e.g., embroidery foot) so the cord feeds through easily. See *News Flash* on page 121.

To make a stitching guideline, fold the first strip in half the long way and finger press the fold. Open the strip flat. Place the fold line under the needle and look at the throat plate to the right of the strip. If a line is etched where the fabric falls, use it as a guide when stitching. If not, then place a piece of Magic Tape next to the strip and stitch over the cord with the right edge of the strips lined up with the tape. Using stitch width 3, stitch length 1-1/2 or 2, stitch from one bias strip to the next without anchoring or knotting (Fig. 5.18). When finished, tie a knot in the end of the cord.

Take the strips to a comfortable chair, sit down, turn on the TV, and make ruffles. Start by pulling up the cord between the first two strips into a loop. Clip the cord in the middle and tie a knot at the top of the second strip. Keep pulling on the cord at the end of the first strip until the ruffle

Fig. 5.18 Zigzag over a cord down the center of each strip.

is as full as you wish. This rug has ruffles in a ratio of one to three. If the strip is 3 feet (.9m) long, gather it to 1 foot (30.5cm). Tie another knot in the cord to hold the gathers in place. Go on to the next strip; pull the cord up between strips 2 and 3. Clip the cord in the middle and tie a knot at the start of strip 3. Pull on the unknotted end of the cord until strip 2 is gathered, tie a knot, and go on to strips 3 and 4. Continue until all the strips are gathered. It's not important that gathers be evenly spaced because you space them later when stitching the ruffles in place.

Place a ruffle on the first stripe at the left edge of the ticking with center stitching positioned over the stripe. Before stitching, fold under approximately 1/4" (6mm) at the beginning of the first ruffle to make a finished edge. Anchor the strip by backstitching to anchor the threads. Then evenly space the gathers along the cord, hold the strip down on the stripe, and zigzag stitch it in place. Line up the next ruffle and stitch it down, without folding under either end. Continue until you get to the other edge of the backing. Cut off any extra ruffle to fit, leaving enough fabric to turn under again at the edge.

Stitch the next row and each of the subsequent rows at least 1/2" (1.5cm) from the previous row of ruffles (Fig. 5.19), pushing the first row's ruffles to the left. If you stitch the rows closer, the rug curls. Use the ticking stripes as guides. When you finish attaching ruffles, the rug is finished—except for clean up.

Place the rug on a hard surface. Are any ruffle edges up too high? None of them is perfectly even with the adjoining strip, but you may find a few above the norm. Clip them off using appliqué or rug (machine embroidery) scissors. Then clip off cord knots and any other cord not caught in the stitching. It's finished—start dancing!

Idea: If you have a ruffle/pleater attachment for your sewing machine, cut the strips 1-1/2" (4cm) wide and run the strips through the attachment to gather them on one side. Attach them to the backing by stitching over the first line of stitches at the side of the ruffle.

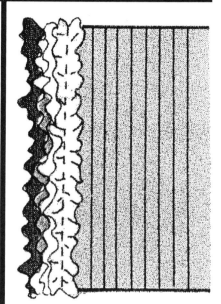

Fig. 5.19

Fig. 5.19 Apply gathered strips to the backing by stitching down the centers.

Chapter V **Scraps and Strips** **119**

Fig. 5.20A

Fig. 5.20B

Fig. 5.21

Fig. 5.22

More shirring ruffles ideas: If you would like more control over design, if you're tired of always stitching in a straight line, I found a rug you'll love. The directions, which I found in an old rug book, are difficult to comprehend. Yet even if I'm doing it wrong (there were no photos and no illustrations), my sample works.

The rug is gathered as if making the Carmen Miranda rug—until you attach the ruffles. (Although in the book long running stitches were used to gather the ruffles, I prepared all my ruffles, as usual, by zigzagging over cordonnet.)

Then the reader is directed to roll the gathered fabric (they used 1/2" (1.5cm) wide bias strips) between the palms to create a "home-manufacture braid." I went as far as rolling the gathered fabric between my palms (and felt pretty foolish—I knew it would never look like any braid I'd ever seen) till I came to my senses, recalled "poetic license," and knew that if the inventor of this rug had had a zigzag machine, this is how the "braid" would be constructed, and it's definitely a time saver: after zigzagging over cordonnet down the center of the strip (I used 2" (5cm) wide strips), I pulled on the cord until the ruffle was gathered tight, then held the ruffle at each end and twisted one end clockwise, the other end counterclockwise. It twisted up into a ball. Then I went back to the book's directions (it told me that the next step "took ingenuity"). I held the tight roll of gathers to a canvas backing fabric. Starting at one end, I gradually loosened up the gathers and, with a hand-needle and thread, I began stitching haphazardly over the cordonnet to couch it down in various spots (all the time I was attaching the ruffle, I kept loosening the roll and deciding just how tightly these ruffles should be drawn up and how close together I should attach them). The book told me to clip the braid for a uniform surface, but my

Fig. 5.20
A. Couch down a cord through the center of the strip.
B. Pull up on the cord and twist one end of the ruffle clockwise, the other end counter-clockwise.

Fig. 5.21 The ruffle is twisted into a ball.

Fig. 5.22 Pull the ruffle out and arrange in a design, while attaching it with hand stitches over the couched cord.

ruffles were acceptable as they were. What a surprise—I loved this technique and saw more possibilites for designing with this than with the machine-attached version, even though the author suggested sewing the braids in straight lines.

I can ruffle any design because I have complete control over the ruffle's placement—it's possible to follow any design line or fill in any space.

Once my ruffle was in place, I yanked on it in several spots and thought there was too much play in some areas so I went over it again and stitched it down here and there where it needed to be attached.

It is fast and easy to manipulate. Flowers, always a popular design motif, yet difficult because of circles and curves, are quickly pushed and pulled into shape by using the cordonnet cord to control the looseness or tightness of the ruffle.

It was fun recreating this old technique. Now will someone out there tell me if I'm doing it right?

More thoughts on ruffles: Have you noticed that this is not only a book of rug ideas, it's also a collection of textures? Because the textures are on a large scale, we may lose sight of other uses for them. Sometimes these interesting ruffles are too heavy for wearables, but if they're made of silk and sheers or even tiny 1/4" (6mm) wide ribbon instead of 2" (5cm) wide strips of cotton, they're adaptable.

Carmen Miranda sleeves need no explanation. I made them out of junky fabric and used them on a costume, but recently I saw shirred strips of organza (sewed slightly farther apart than on the rug or the costume) made into puffed sleeves on a formal gown. Beautiful!

Try gathering narrow ribbons in the same way, then attaching them to garments (it's called ruching). Attach the ruching with beads or try a decorative stitch on your sewing machine. Jane Hill decorates socks with ruching. Above all, use ingenuity.

News Flash!

As we went to press, a student in my rug class made a discovery. Darla Grimes of St. Petersburg, Florida, eliminated the need for zigzagging over gimp when she used the gathering foot to produce evenly shirred, gorgeous ruffles.

Place the gathering foot on top of and in the middle of the strip you're gathering. Tension must be increased to the highest number, or whatever your machine needs to closely gather fabric strips. Straight stitch down the center of the strip (stitch length a long 4 or basting length). Always experiment with both tension and stitch length before you begin. The gathers should be close, but not tight—see cover photo.

Butt strips up to each other (don't overlap them) as you progress and don't join strips of the same pattern or color. This "mile-long" gathered strip is then sewn directly to the backing.

It's true that some machines don't have a gathering foot. However, in some cases you may be able to use a gathering foot from another machine by combining it with an adaptor shank or ankle that fits your machine. Ask your dealer to help you.

Chapter V **Scraps and Strips** **121**

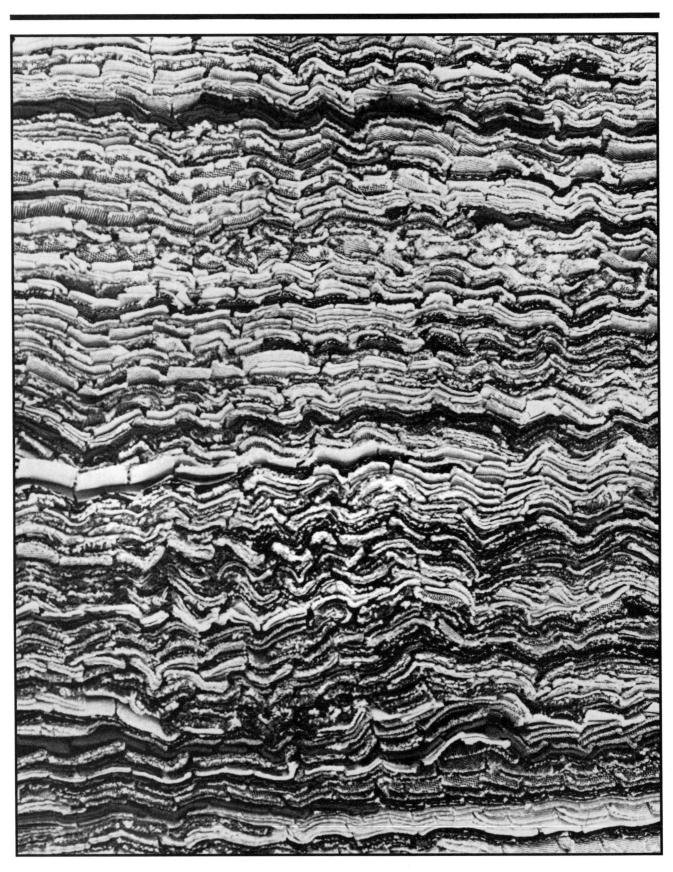

19. Denim Chenille Mat

T his little mat eats up yards of fabric. I used old jeans, together with denim remnants I picked up at sales, and kept cutting 2-1/2" (6.5cm) strips on the bias until I had finished the rug.

Mat size: 16" X 24" (40.6cm X 61cm)

Stitch width: 0

Stitch length: 2

Needle position: left

Needle: #90/14 jeans

Presser foot: zipper

Fabric suggestion: 2-1/2" (6.5cm) bias strips of blue and red denim—as many as needed to cover the surface (use remnants and old jeans); 18" X 26" (46cm X 66cm) heavy canvas fabric to back rug

Thread: polyester sewing thread to match

For the rug backing, you'll need a piece of heavy canvas. Use Method 1 in Appendix A to finish the rug.

Finger press the first bias strip the long way to find the center, but open it again and place it 1/8" (3mm) from the left side of the backing. With zipper foot on, needle left, sew down the strips from top to bottom, stitching in that center crease (Fig. 5.23A). Fold the right side of the strip to the left. Push the next strip as close as you can get it to the first. Sew down the center (Fig. 5.23B). If you run out of fabric for a strip, add another by overlapping the last strip at least an inch.

When you finish, clip every strip every 1" (2.5cm), staggering the clips from row to row (Fig. 5.24). Wash and dry the rug to soften it.

This becomes a heavy rug to maneuver on the machine. To make a larger one, stitch up modules, then join them.

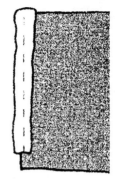

Fig. 5.23A

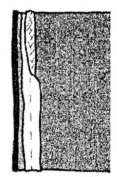

Fig. 5.23B

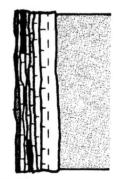

Fig. 5.24

Fig. 5.23
   A. Straight stitch down the center of each bias strip to attach it to the backing.
   B. Flip the right side of the strip to the left and attach the next strip.

Fig. 5.24 Clip strips every 1" (2.5cm), then stagger the clips on the subsequent strips.

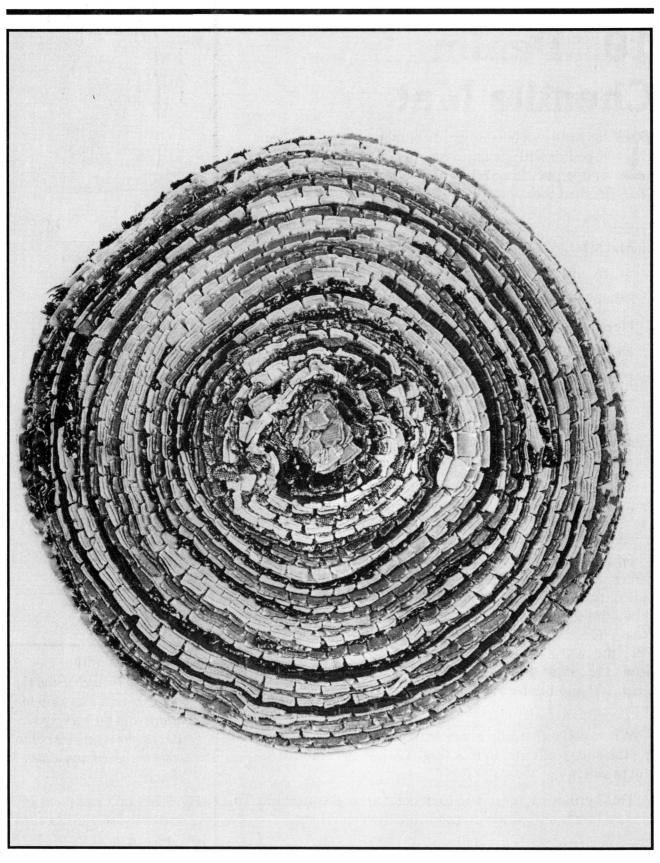

20. Flat Folds and Clipped Strips Chair Rug

T he following is a fabric fringe project created without a fringe fork. I cut up old jeans because I have boxes of them, but you could use any heavy fabric. After cutting the strips, I made a sample piece to determine how closely together I wanted to stitch the rows.

Rug size: 16" (40.5cm) diameter

Stitch width: optional

Stitch length: optional

Needle: #110/18 jeans

Thread: light blue polyester on top and bobbin

Presser foot: general purpose

Fabric suggestion: 2 -1/2" (6.5cm) blue and red bias strips—the length of the strip does not matter; one or two 17" (43cm) diameter canvas circles (see directions)

Miscellaneous: rotary cutter, mat, 6" X 24" (15cm X 61cm) clear plastic ruler, fabric shears, hand-sewing needle

Wash and dry any new fabric you use. Finish the backing using Method 1 or 2 in Appendix A. With the ruler, rotary cutter, and mat, measure and cut 2-1/2" (6.5cm) bias strips. The bias strips are folded in half the long way, wrong sides together, and placed on the outside of the circle, starting an inch from the edge of the foundation fabric. The fold of the bias strips are on the edge of the backing and the raw edges of the rug are off the backing. Place the needle at the fold. Without pulling on the strips—you know how bias will stretch—stitch the strips around the circle. Use a straight stitch or narrow zigzag. Each strip will be about 1/4" (6mm) in from the one previous to it in the circle (Fig. 5.25).

Denim comes in many different colors of blue. Take advantage of this and vary the colors as you add strips to the circle. To add strips, stop an inch from the end of the strip you're stitching, overlap it by placing the new strip on top of the previous one, and continue stitching. Every once in a while stitch in a red strip.

Clip the denim as you sew, cutting into the strip almost to the stitching line every 1/2" (1.5cm). The clips in adjacent rows are like shingles on a roof—no two clips together. The circle may dome up—especially if it is small, but clipping helps flatten it. Sew as far as you can near the center. Then stitch the last few inches by hand. After completing the rug, I put it into the washer and dryer several times to soften the edges.

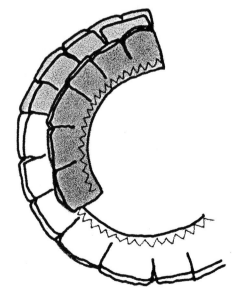

Fig. 5.25 Fold bias strips and apply to round rug backing. Clip as you stitch to keep the rug flat.

Fig. 5.25

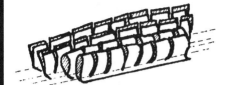

Fig. 5.26

I saw an interesting variation of this rug in a renovated home. From ceiling to floor, the owners had kept the flavor of an earlier day. The rug that interested me the most was made from felt strips, which had been sewn into tubes (see Ravel Rug), straight stitched to a backing, and then clipped into loops. Some of those loops were cut through at the top fold to create fringe. The rug maker had accomplished the same look as the denim chair mat, but instead of stitching down the fold and fringing, the strip was stitched at the cut edge and then cut into loops and fringes. The more I study the differences in rugs, the more I see similarities.

Either of the previous methods is used on the shaggy shirts, coats, even skirts that are in fashion now. The fringe on clothing is usually 100% cotton so when the garment is washed, the fringe scrunches up, rolls, and frays, which is exactly the look you want to achieve. I sew strips of fringe to kids' socks, too—especially if I've decorated a matching sweatshirt with fringe. These fringes would be wonderful on a pair of Margaret Bowman's boots (see Ravel Rug, page 41). Go really wild with them and cover a duffle bag or be timid and use them on a tote.

Fig. 5.27

Fig. 5.26 Felt tubes are sewn to a felt backing on an antique rug. The tubes are cliped into loops and fringes.

Fig. 5.27 Fabric fringe is often used on clothing today.

Fig. 5.28

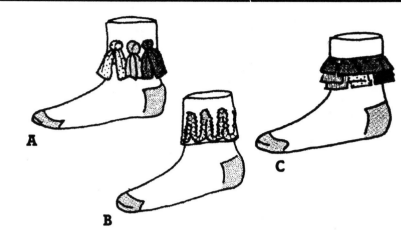

Fig. 5.29

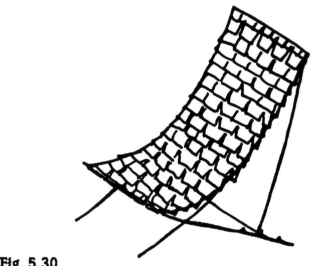

Fig. 5.30

Fig. 5.28 Fabric fringe is often used on clothing today.

Fig. 5.29 Decorate socks with fabric scraps of:
  A. Square knots.
  B. Ruching.
  C. Fabric fringe. Attach colorful strips to a sweatshirt by stitching through the centers of the strips, then tying them into knots.

Fig. 5.30 Fabric fringe a sling chair.

Afterword

The rug variations I can make on a sewing machine amaze me, and I've only scratched the surface in this book. But I hope I've inspired you to experiment and discover new textures and rug methods on your own. Try using different kinds of fabrics, sizes of scraps, weights of yarn. Clip, copy, or sketch, rug and texture ideas from magazines and books and start your own rug file. Then, don't use your creative inventions for rugs only. Use your file when you need a special idea for a unique gift, one-of-a-kind clothing, accessories, or home decor. You're only limited by your imagination.

Appendix A

Finishing Rugs

Although you may not think it necessary to finish the underside of your rugs to look as good as the top side (after all, who will see it and who cares?), I have three reasons why I often do and why you may want to. First, I don't often clip every thread as I go along. Call me messy—I admit it—but that's how I sew rugs and one reason why I can make them as fast as I do—especially when I know I'm going to cover them anyway.

But I put on a backing for a more important reason than covering up the mess. I cover the stitches so they'll wear better. That's my second reason—the rug lasts longer.

Another reason for putting on a second backing is stability. With two backings, the rug lays better, and those pesky ends that may want to curl can't.

Of course you can add backing later if the rug is too skittish, or the corners start to curl later. Fold in a couple of inches around the perimeter of a piece of canvas to match the size of the rug you're backing. Fuse down the fold-over or stitch it in place with a whip stitch. You can also use press-on Velcro dots to keep the two backings together while in use. If you make the backing removable, the rug isn't as heavy or unrelenting when you wash it.

Following are three finishing methods I used to finish each of the rugs in this book. I sometimes use removable double backings with Methods 1 and 3 (if my rug is for a gift I whip stitch the backing to the rug to make it more attractive and more permanent). Method 2 already has a double backing.

Method 1.

The cutting dimensions of the rug backing should be enlarged by 2" (5cm) in width and length over its finished size. (The cutting dimensions are given for each rug in this book under "Fabric.") Then use a marker or pencil (the lines won't show) and a ruler to mark 1" (2.5cm) within all four edges of the fabric you've chosen as the backing. Straight stitch all around the backing on these lines using the same color thread as your backing. Fold toward the top side on the side lines first and zigzag within the fold, then again at the inside edge (Fig. A.1A). Do the same along the top and bottom. The rug is finished before it's begun!

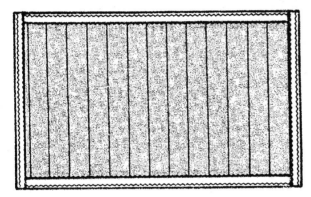

Fig. A.1A

An alternative to this uses 1" (2.5cm) strips of Perky Bond or Stitch Witchery fusible webbing. Fuse the webbing all around the edges between the edge and the stitched line, fold on the stitching line and fuse the edge to the fabric: no need to stitch in place (Fig. A.1B).

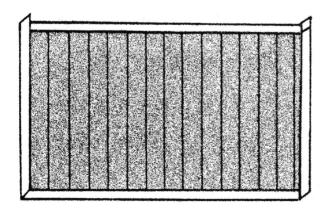

Fig. A.1B

Fig. A.1 Method 1
  A. Fold back edges to the top side.
  B. Press fusibles between folded edge and topside of the backing, or zigzag edge to attach.

If your rug is round or oval, add 1" (2.5cm) at the finished edge. Then draw a line 1" (2.5cm) from the edge and stitch on the line. Clip the edge every few inches (centimeters) (Fig. A.2A) and fold it back toward the top side. Dot glue under the folds with glue stick; then stitch around the backing at the fold on the edge (Fig. A.2B).

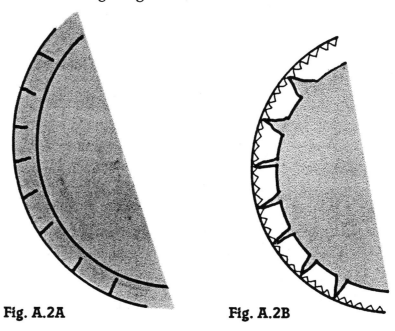

Fig. A.2A

Fig. A.2B

Fig. A.2 Method 1 for circular rugs
    A. Clip in around edge of circle to 1" (2.5cm) line.
    B. Fold and press on line to the topside, glue and zigzag in place.

Method 2.

For the cutting size of the backing, add 2" (5cm) to the finished measurements. Mark a line 1" (2.5cm) inside the cut edge all around the backing. Straight stitch on the markings around the rug. As you construct the rug, don't stitch beyond the 1" (2.5cm) border. When the rug is completed, cut another backing the same size as the first and pin it, right sides together, to the rug. Be sure none of the yarn or fabric decoration is caught in the seam as you stitch around three sides. Use the zipper foot to nudge close to the rug decoration inside. When straight stitching is completed, go back and zigzag outside the straight stitching. Leave the top edge open (Fig. A.3A).

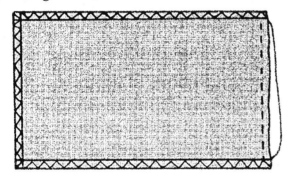

Fig. A.3A

Turn the rug right side out—it looks like a pillow case. Smooth it down and turn the border inside at the open edge (Fig. A.3B). Hand stitch it in place, or take it to the machine and stitch across it at the folds (if there is enough space). You may want to go one step further by tacking the top to the backing. If the rug has been constructed in strips, stitch down between the strips.

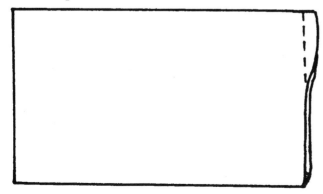

Fig. A.3B

Fig. A.3 Method 2
  A. Topsides together, attach second backing to finished rug by straight stitching around 3 sides, then zigzagging the edges.
  B. Turn right side out, then fold in edge and hand-stitch together.

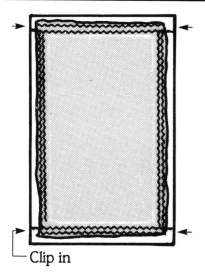

Clip in

Fig. A.4A

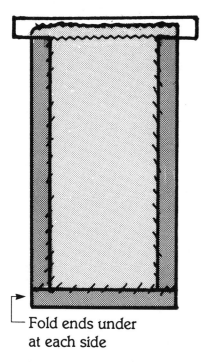

Fold ends under
at each side

Fig. A.4B

Method 3.

Rug binding or tape is available from craft stores in colors (or see Sources of Supplies). Find one 1-1/4" (3.2cm) wide or wider to match or come close to the color of the backing of your rug. Wash the tape to preshrink it. On the top side of the rug, match a long edge of the binding to the last stitched row. The binding will extend beyond the raw edge. Begin and end 1" (2.5cm) from the raw edges of the top and bottom. Zigzag the inside edge of the binding. Turn the rug over and zigzag again at the edge of the backing.

Repeat for the rug binding across the top and bottom extending the binding the entire way (Fig. A.4A). When the rug is completed, clip between the top and side tapes (to the marked line) without cutting any zigzag threads. Do the same at the bottom. Turn under the tape at the sides and hand stitch in place with heavy-duty thread (Fig. A.4B). Turn the top and bottom over and hand stitch in place. Turn in at the side corners and hand stitch down in place.

An iron-on rug binding is also available. Use it for shag-type rugs where edges are covered with yarn fringes or fabric scraps.

Fig. A.4 Method 3
  A. Attach rug binding to sides, then top and bottom.
  B. Clip between tapes, then fold tape back to the underside and attach by hand.

Cut two lengths as long as the sides of the rug. Then crease the binding in half the long way and slip the rug in (Fig. A.5A). Iron down on the topside, then turn the rug over and iron the backside for a good bond.

Cut two lengths for the top and bottom sides, adding 4" per side to the lengths. Crease in half lengthwise, slip the rug in with 2" (5cm) extending at each end, and bond as before—but don't bond the extensions. Cut along the crease of the binding from the extension to the edge of the rug. Remove the binding on back that extends beyond the rug edge. Fold the remaining binding to the back of the rug and iron in place (Fig. A.5B).

To protect your stitching and the rug itself, place a thin foam rubber or the gridlike rubber pad underneath your rug, cutting it 1" (2.5cm) shorter and narrower than your rug. Not only is the rug softer to step on, but it won't slip. These are available in craft stores and through many mail-order companies (see Sources of Supplies).

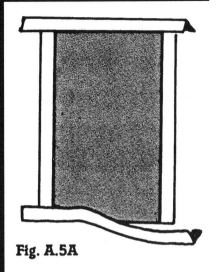

Fig. A.5A

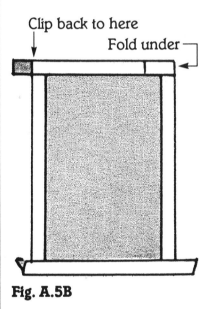

Clip back to here

Fold under

Fig. A.5B

Fig. A.5 Iron-on rug binding tape is an alternative:
A. Slip edges of rug backing into folded bindings.
B. Clip out the back of tape extensions at each side of the top and bottom edges, fold back the tape and press in place.

Appendix A **Finishing Rugs** **135**

Appendix B

Rug Care

Throw-rugs should be easy to clean so I make most of these rugs washable. All the fabrics you use on rugs, whether on top or the backings, should be prewashed. Then, when you wash the rugs later, there won't be any surprises. However, if there is a question in your mind, then remove your rugs from the washing machine either right before a spin cycle (although I doubt there are many rugs too fragile for a spin cycle) or right after the spin cycle.

If you remove the rug before all the rinse water is out of it, roll it up and squeeze out the water by hand or foot. We have a basement with a drain in the floor, a perfect spot to squish the water out of a rug, but you can always take it outside on a warm day.

When removing the rug after the spin cycle, pull the rug out of the washer and into shape, leaving it to dry flat (I have a couple of old blankets I spread on the freezer or table to use for drying sweaters and rugs). Don't hang your rugs to dry because they'll probably dry out of shape, and the weight may break stitches.

Fluff the rugs on "air dry" later, if necessary.

If you used the fabrics I suggested, then the following rugs can be washed in warm water and dried in a warm to cool dryer: T-shirt knit, Amish Dustcatcher, Squares and Triangles, Quilted Bath Mat, both Cheater's and Instant Rugs, and both denim rugs. If the yarn you use for the yarn rugs is polyester or acrylic, as mine are, then those are safe, too.

Unless you use all linen-like fabrics that dry smoothly, wash the Fringed Linen Rug, but dry it by pulling the backing into shape on a flat surface, smoothing out the fringes, then later tossing it in the dryer to fluff up the fringe after it's dry. Canvas and ticking fabrics dry wrinkled and stiff so you may want to take any rug out of the dryer while it is still possible to pull the backing into shape, then let it dry on a flat surface. Depending on the nature of the rug, this is not always necessary. And, with repeated washing and drying, the backing softens and lies flat.

The Carmen Miranda Rug, Caterpillar, and Fabric Fringe Rugs are treated like the Fringed Linen rug unless you used blends. If you did, then toss them into the washer and dryer to clean. The Shirred Carmen Miranda Rug, like the Denim Chenille Mat, looks better after repeated washing and drying.

Often the size and weight of the rug—especially when wet—is too much for your own machine. Simply take it to a laundromat that has large-load machines.

The black Coiled Craft Cord rug can be vacuumed regularly and cleaned with a spray-type carpet cleaner. When spots appear on the Snowflake Rug or the Welcome Mat, treat them immediately with a damp cloth or spray carpet cleaner, but for overall cleaning, send them to the dry cleaners.

Vacuum the Plaid Ravel Mat with a brush attachment so the long yarn ends aren't caught and pulled into the vacuum, but for general cleaning, send it to a professional carpet cleaner.

The bottom line is to understand the properties of the fabrics you use. Prewashing and drying them tells you how the rugs will look later. Remember the samples I asked you to do? Experiment on those before you begin your rug. The results will convince you to do the cleaning yourself, or to send your rug out to a dry cleaner or carpet cleaner.

Appendix C

History of Handmade Rugs in America

We assume that rugs have always been used on floors. Not so. In the fifteenth century, and perhaps long before that, the "ryijy" or rugs of Finland were used for bed coverings. The word *rugge* meant "coarse" or "rough"; in Swedish and Norwegian it meant a coarse coverlet. In English it meant "thick cloak" or "coarse material" and was defined in a dictionary then as a shaggy coverlet for a bed.

The colonists used rugs on beds, also. In fact, until 1820, *rugg* meant coarse woolen cloth or bedcover. Most rugs into the first part of the nineteenth century were bed rugs or were used to cover furniture. Also, the rugs decorated walls to keep out drafts. Fabric was precious and scarce and not used on the floor until it was useless for anything else. Then the rugs were made of pieces of overlapped, worn-out clothing applied to homespun.

By the end of the eighteenth century, colonists used painted canvas floor cloths. Indeed, rag rugs weren't in wide use until the mid-1800s.

Time Line of Handmade Rugs

1700

    canvas floor cloths

1800

    to 1835—bed rugs embroidered with tent and cross stitches

    appliqué and patchwork rugs

    to 1840—yarn-sewn bed rugs made at home (running stitch)

    floor cloths of canvas

1830

imported woven carpets

rugs were small and made either at home or by itinerant local weavers (rag carpets made from cloth strips)

also appliquéd and embroidered at home, shirred

(appliqué type), bias shirred rugs, braided

1840

woven rugs in use—also hooked, shirred, and sewn

to 1860—caterpillar rugs

bias cut strips, gathered to stand at right angles

bias cut, shirred—two or three strips together

strips cut with grain, gathered and sewn to lie flat in overlapping rows

1850

to late 1800's—hooked, shag, knitted and crocheted

use of burlap backing, introduction of stamped (commercial) rug

1890

to early twentieth century—penny, ravel rugs (few families without rugs.)

1900

linoleum is popular—rugs not used as much

Sources of Supplies

Threads

Note: Ask your local retailer or send a pre-addressed stamped envelope to the companies below to find out where to buy their threads.

DMC 100% cotton, Sizes 30 and 50, pearl cotton:

The DMC Corporation
107 Trumbull Street
Elizabeth, NJ 07206

Dual-Duty Plus Extra-fine, cotton-wrapped polyester:

Coats & Clark
30 Patewood Plaza
Greenville, SC 29615

Mettler Metrosene Fine Machine Embroidery cotton, Size 60/2, Cordonnet:

Swiss-Metrosene, Inc.
c/o Wm. E. Wright Co.
W. Warren, MA 04864

Sewing Machine Supplies

(Write for catalogs)

Aardvark Adventures
PO Box 2449
Livermore, CA 94550
(Threads, yarn, tassel maker)

The Button Shop
PO Box 1065
Oak Park, IL 60304
(Presser feet)

Clotilde Inc.
237 SW 28th St.
Ft. Lauderdale, FL 33315
(Presser feet, thread and much more)

Nancy's Notions
PO Box 683
Beaver Dam, WI 53916
(Sirco sewing table and much more)

Sewing Emporium
1087 Third Avenue
Chula Vista, CA 92010
(Presser feet, accessories)

Speed Stitch, Inc.
PO Box 3472
Port Charlotte, FL 33952
(Sewing supplies)

Miscellaneous

(Write for catalogs)

Boycan's Craft and Art Supplies
PO Box 897
Sharon, PA 16146

Cabin Fever Calicoes
PO Box 54
Center Sandwich, NH 03227

Clearbrook Woolen Shop
PO Box 8
Clearbrook, VA 22624

The Fabric Carr
PO Box 32120
San Jose, CA 95152

Home-Sew
Bethlehem, PA 18018
(Sewing accessories)

Lee Ward (Hdqtrs.)
840 N. State Street
Elgin, IL 60120
(Yarn, thread, rug supplies. Local stores—no mail order)

The Perfect Notion
115 Maple St.
Toms River, NJ 08753

Salem Industries, Inc.
PO Box 43027
Atlanta, GA 30336
(Olfa cutters, rulers)

Solar-Kist Corp.
PO Box 273
La Grange, IL 60525
(Teflon pressing sheet)

Magazines

(Write for rates)

Aardvark Territorial Enterprise
PO Box 2449
Livermore, CA 94550
(Newspaper jammed with all kinds of information about all kinds of embroidery, design, threads, books, and things to order); I ordered the tasselmaker from them.

Fiberarts
50 College St.
Asheville, NC 28801
(Gallery of the best fiber artists, including those who work in machine stitchery)

Sew News
PO Box 1790
Peoria, IL 61656
(Monthly tabloid includes home decorating)

Threads
Box 355
Newton, CT 06470
(Magazine on all fiber crafts)

Treadleart
25834 Narbonne Ave., Ste. 1
Lomita, CA 90717
(Magazine and catalog of supplies)

Yarn

(Write for catalog or information)

Lily Craft Products
B. Blumenthal & Co., Inc.
Carlstadt, NJ 07072
(Sugar 'n Cream cotton yarn)

Rug Supplies

(Write for catalogs)

The Cord Co.
5611 Virginia
Kansas City, MO 64110
(Cord samples)

Dorr Mill Store
Box 88
Guild, NH 03754
(Wool in solid colors; $3/2 color charts)

Dritz Corp.
Spartanburg, SC 29304
(Iron-on rug binding)

Earth Guild
One Tingle Alley
Asheville, NC 28801
(Mill ends, books, samples)

Great Northern Weaving
PO Box 361
Augusta, MI 49012
(Roping, rug filler, cotton warp, books, samples, supplies, equipment)

The Nantucket Collection
Heather Hill Farm
PO Box 1089
N. Charlestown, NH 03603
(Rugs & kits)

Oriental Rug Co.
214 S. Central Ave.
PO Box 917
Lima, OH 45802
(Samples, books)

Rafter-four Designs
PO Box 3056
Sandpoint, Idaho 83864
($2 catalog, books, supplies, kits. This is a unique catalog—Diana Blake Gray introduces you to every type of rug imaginable)

The Ruggery
565 Cedar Swamp Road
Glen Head, NY 11545
(Books, yarn, backings, cord, equipment)

Whitin Yarns
47 Water Street
PO Box 937
Norwalk, Conn.
(Yarn samples)

Wilde Yarns
3737 Main Street
Philadelphia, PA 19127
(Samples)

Book Mail-Order

Hard-to-Find Needlework Books
Bette Feinstein
96 Roundwood Road
Newton, MA 02164
(Textile books and magazines)

Wooden Porch Books
Rt.1, Box 262
Middlebourne, WV 26149
(Textile books, $3/3 catalogs of out-of-print needlework books)

Bibliography

Note: Although many of these books are out-of-print, your public library may be able to borrow them for you through Interlibrary Loan.

Allen, Doris, *Handmade Rugs*, Lane Publishing Co., 1953.

Allison, Linda and Stella, *Rags*, Clarkson N. Potter, Inc., 1979.

Batchelder, Martha, *Art of Hooked-rug Making*, Manual Arts Press, 1947.

Bath, Virginia, *Needlework in America*, Viking Press, 1979.

Beitler, Ethel Jane, *Hooked and Knotted Rugs*, Sterling Publishing Co., Inc., 1973.

Better Homes & Gardens *Traditional American Crafts*, Meredith Corp., 1988.

Evrard, Gwen, *Twinkletoes Footgear to Make and Wear*, Scribner's and Sons, 1976.

Gordon, Beverly, *Shaker Textile Arts*, University Press of New England, 1980.

Hinchliffe, John, and Angela Jeffs, *Rugs from Rags*, Brook House Publishers, Inc., 1977.

Johnson, Mary Elizabeth, *Rugs*, Oxmoor House, 1979.

Katz, Ruth J., *Footwear*, Van Nostrand Reinhold Co., 1979.

Knopf, *Collector's Guide to Quilts, Coverlets, Rugs & Samplers*, American Antiques, 1982.

Koenig and Spiers, *Making Rugs for Pleasure & Profit*, Arco Publishing Inc., 1980.

Kopp, Joel and Kate, *American Hooked & Sewn Rug*, E. P. Dutton & Co., 1975.

Laury, Jean Ray and Joyce Aiken, *Handmade Rugs from Practically Anything*, Countryside Press, 1972.

Macbeth, Ann, *The Country Woman's Rug Book*, Manual Arts Press, 1971.

Marein, Shirley, *Creating Rugs and Wall Hangings*, Studio Vista Publishers, Viking Press, 1975.

Meany, Janet and Paula Pfaff, *Rag Rug Handbook*, Dos Tejedoras Fiber Arts Publication, 1988.

Meilach, Dona Z., *Making Contemporary Rugs and Wall-hangings*, Abelard-Schuman Ltd., 1970.

Picken, Mary Brooks, *Singer Sewing Book*, Singer Sewing Machine Co., 1949.

Rag Rugs, Search Press, 1980

Ries, Estelle H., *American Rugs*, World Publishing Co.,

Safford, Carleton L. and Robert Bishop, *America's Quilts & Coverlets*, E.P. Dutton & Co., Inc., 1972.

Silver, Lona, *Rugs from Rags*, Drake Publisher's Inc., 1976.

Von Rosenstiel, Helene, *American Rugs & Carpets*, William Morrow & Co., Inc., 1978.

Znamierowski, Nell, *Step-by-step Rugmaking*, Golden Press, 1972.

Index

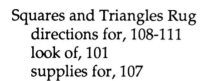